CW01509673

RAVEN TALES

Stories of the Raven based on the folklore of the Tlingit, Haida, Tsimshian, Inuit, and Athapascan of Alaska

DENNIS WALLER

Front cover image courtesy of Angel Ortiz

Angel Ortiz - Fine Art fineartamerica.com

https://www.facebook.com/Angelwints

DEDICATION

A special thanks to Dr. Franz Boas and John R. Swanton for their hard work that started over a hundred years ago. Their dedication and commitment to preserve the heritage and history of the Tlingit and Haida still lives on today, Thank you gentlemen!

Thank you Sean Asiqłuq Topkok with the Alaska Native Knowledge Network and University of Alaska Fairbanks for blessing me with the honor of having my works made available to share through their exchange program. http://www.ankn.uaf.edu/

Thank You Angel Ortiz for your use of your artwork! You have captured the essence of the tales

CONTENTS

ACKNOWLEDGMENTS

Long ago, even before the days of the animal people the world was only a great ocean where there was no land or any living thing except a great Bird. The Bird, after a long, long time, flew down to the surface of the water and dipped his great black wings into the flood. The earth arose out of the waters. So began the creation. While the land was still soft, the first man burst from the pod of the beach pea and looked out upon the endless plain behind him and the gray salt sea before him. He was the only man. Then Raven appeared to him and the creation of other beings began. Raven made also animals for food and clothing. Later, because the earth plain was so bare, he planted trees and shrubs and grass and set the green things to growing.

With creation by a Great Spirit, there came dangers from evil spirits. Such spirits carried away the sun and moon, and hung them to the rafters of the dome-shaped Alaskan huts. The world became cold and cheerless, and in the Land of Darkness white skins became blackened by contact with the darkness. So it became necessary to search for the sun and hang it again in the dome-shaped sky above them. Darkness in the Land of Long Night was the cause, through magic, of the bitter winds of winter — winds which came down from the North, bringing with them ice and cold and snow. This was the work of some Great Spirit which had loosened the side of the gray cloud-tent under which they lived, letting in the bitter winds of another world. Spirits blow the mists over the cold north sea so that canoes lose sight of their home-land. Spirits also drive the ice floes, with their fishermen, far over the horizon of ocean, into the still colder North. Spirits govern the run of the salmon, the catching of whales, and all the life of the people of the North who wage such a terrific struggle for existence.

So there must be those who have power over the evil spirits, those who by incantations and charms of magic, by ceremonial dancing in symbolic dress, can control the designs of those who work ever against these children of the North. Thus there arose the shamans with all their ceremonies.- Katharine Berry Judson

i

CHAPTER ONE
RAVEN AND HIS TALES

The Raven is as much a paradoxical creature as he is important in the myths of many native cultures. The central character of these stories, the Raven, is considered the benevolent creator, filling the world with beauty and harmony, the master mind behind all that is good and looked upon with warm admiration.

On the other hand, he is often viewed as a malevolent conniving, scheming trickster with self-gratification as his only goal. There are stories of the Raven eating the unsuspecting victim out of house and home or bidding someone to do his work, or indiscriminately seducing someone for a sexual tryst, man or woman I might add. With all of this said, even regarded as a spoiled man-child with a petulance towards childish behavior, he is still the ultimate larger-than-life heroic figure within the myths.

Whether it is creating animals, chasing down a woman to marry, or looking for a meal, one thing is for sure, the Tales of the Raven has left us with a rich and colorful history recorded in the myths and legends of the indigenous people.

While the Raven appears throughout the world in mythology, such as the raven was the first bird to leave Noah's Ark as well as being in Norse mythology as a pair of ravens that traveled the world every day in order to keep Odin informed of current events to probably the most famous raven tale being the poem, "Nevermore" by Edgar Alan Poe. Our focus here will be centered on the Tlingit, Tsimshian, Haida, the Yupiit and Inupiat also known as the Inuit, and the Athapascan Peoples of Alaska.

What follows are 30 stories that seem to contradict each other adding to the confusion as to what or who this Raven really is. The cornerstone of this book are the Creation Stories of the Tlingit, Haida, and the Inuit which shows why the Raven is regarded as a grandfather to the people and is thought of with respect in asking for good health, good hunting, and for good fortune. It was the Raven that created man, the forest and the animals that inhabited them, the rivers and the fish that live in the water. In this context, the Raven is revered.

However there are other stories that portray the Raven as a lazy scavenger, living off the hard work of others, or seeking sexual pleasure, the Raven is a shining example of how multi-faceted a myth can be. From being worship to being considered a lazy birdbrained (pardon the pun) imbecile, the Raven has most definitely left us with a fascinating collection of tales. At the very least, I hope you'll find these entertaining and enlightening into the minds and hearts of the indigenous people of Alaska.

Is any of this real?

The question I get more than any other is, "Are these creatures real?" This question misses the point in my opinion. The fact remains that these stories about the Raven, Kushtaka, Buk-wus, Gonaqadet and others are real. Many of them have been passed down for hundreds, maybe thousands of years through an oral tradition. An interesting quote I read from a Tlingit was, "The Tlingit and the Haida don't have myths; they are stories about our history." I believe that sums it up nicely.

If you can read between the lines of these tales, and can hear what isn't being said, I think you'll see a subtle revealing of their beliefs, values, and the inner thoughts of a rather advanced people. Just because there is no empirical evidence to support any of the tales, it doesn't necessarily mean that there isn't any truth to them. In reality, these tales may have roots in reality. Given that new species of plant and animal life is being discovered on a daily basis, who is to say that there isn't such thing as the Kushtaka. Legends that have endured for centuries, have endured for a reason.

One of the fascinating aspects of mythology is the similarities of these myths worldwide. There is a universal thread to all of these stories, one that cannot be dismissed. Is it an inherent side of human nature that we keep these tales alive? Are these age old tales a way for man to rationalize and compartmentalize phenomena that is beyond our understanding? Or is a method to bring order out of the chaos? Or just maybe, these people did in fact experience these events and they could only describe or explain them within the framework of their knowledge.

The paradox to all of this is our insatiable need to know what we don't understand and the desire to master the unknown. However, one thought to keep in mind when diving into these myths and legends is to simply remember that every story has worth and value. Maybe along the way, the meaning or symbology has been lost, but that doesn't diminish the value. Besides, it is these mysterious encounters with the unexplainable that makes life interesting, in our need to learn and discover the truth. Remember to listen, to hear with an open mind and maybe perhaps, you'll discover another world out there.

CHAPTER TWO
THE INUIT CREATION STORY

It was in the time when there were no people on the earth plain. The first man for four days lay coiled up in the pod of the beach pea. On the fifth day he stretched out his feet and burst the pod. He fell to the ground and when he stood up he was a full-grown man. Man looked all around him and then at himself. He moved his hands and arms, his neck and legs. When he looked back he saw, still hanging to the vine, the pod of the beach pea, with a hole in the lower end out of which he had dropped. When he looked about him again, he saw that he was getting farther from his starting place. The ground seemed to move up and down under his feet, and it was very soft. After a while he had a strange feeling in his stomach, so he stooped down to drink some water from a small pool at his feet. Then he felt better.

When Man looked up again he saw coming toward him, with a fluttering motion, something dark. He watched the dark thing until it stopped just in front of him. It was Raven.

As soon as Raven stopped, he raised one of his wings and pushed up his beak, as though it were a mask, to the top of his head. Thus Raven changed at once into a man. Raven stared hard at Man, moving from side to side to see him better.

Raven said, "What are you? Where did you come from? I have never seen anything like you."

Raven still stared at Man, surprised to find this new thing so much like himself. He made Man walk around a little, while he turned his head from side to side to see him better.

Then Raven said again, in astonishment, "Where did you come from? I have never seen anything like you before."

Man said, "I came from the pea pod." He pointed to the plant from which he came.

"Ah, I made that vine," said Raven. "But I did not know that anything like you would come from it. Come with me to the high ground over there; it is thicker and harder. This ground I made later and it is soft and thin."

So Man and Raven walked to the higher ground which was firm and hard. Raven asked Man if he had eaten anything. Man said he had taken some of the soft stuff from one of the pools.

"Ah, you drank some water," said Raven. "Now wait for me here."

Raven drew down his beak, as though it were a mask, over his face. He at once became a bird and flew far up into the sky — far out of sight. Man waited until the fourth day. Then Raven returned bringing four berries in his claws. He pushed up his beak and so became a man again. Then he gave to Man two salmon berries and two heath berries, saying, "Here is something I made for you to eat. I wish them to be plentiful on the earth. Eat them."

Man put the berries into his mouth, one after the other, and ate them. Then he felt better. Then Raven left Man near a small creek while he went to the edge of the water. He took two pieces of clay at the water's edge, and shaped them like a pair of mountain sheep. He held them in his hand until they were dry, and then he called Man to come and see them. Man said they were pretty, so Raven told him to close his eyes. Man closed his eyes tightly. Then Raven pulled down his beak-mast, and waved his wings four times over the pieces of clay. At once they bounded away as full-grown mountain sheep. Raven told Man to look.

Man was so much pleased that Raven said, "If these animals are plentiful, perhaps people will try to kill them."

Man said, "Yes."

Then Raven said, "Well, it will be better for them to live among the steep rocks so every one cannot kill them. There only shall they be found."

Raven took two more pieces of clay and shaped them like tame reindeer. He held them in his hand until they were partly dry, then told Man to look at them. Raven again drew down his beak-mask and waved his wings four times over them. Thus they became alive, but as they were only dry in spots while Raven held them, therefore they remained brown and white, with mottled coat. Raven told Man these tame reindeer would be very few in number.

Again Raven took two pieces of clay and shaped them like the caribou or wild reindeer. But he held them in his hands only a little while so that only the bellies of the reindeer became dry and white. Then Raven drew down his beak-mask, and waved his wings over them, and they bounded away. But because only their bellies were dry and white while Raven held them, therefore the wild reindeer is brown except its white belly. Raven said to Man, "These animals will be very common. People will kill many of them."

Thus Raven began to create the animals.

Raven said one day to Man, "You are lonely by yourself. I

will make you a companion." He went to some white clay at a spot distant from the clay of which he had made animals, and made of the clay a figure almost like Man. Raven kept looking at Man while he shaped the figure. Then he took fine water grass from the creek and fastened it on the back of the head for hair. When the clay was shaped, Raven drew down his beak-mask and waved his wings over it. The clay became a beautiful girl. The girl was white and fair because Raven let the clay dry entirely before he waved his wings over it.

Raven took the girl to Man. "There is a companion for you," he said.

Now in the days of the first people on the earth plain, there were no mountains far or near. No rain ever fell and there were no winds. The sun shone always very brightly.

Then Raven showed the first people on the earth plain how to sleep warmly in the dry moss when they were tired. Raven himself drew down his beak-mask and went to sleep like a bird.

When Raven awakened, he went back to the creek. Here he made two sticklebacks, two graylings, and two blackfish. When these were swimming about in the water, he called Man to see them. Man raised his hand in surprise and the sticklebacks darted away. Raven told him the graylings would be found in clear mountain streams, while the sticklebacks would live along the coast, and that both would be good for food.

Raven next made the shrewmouse. He said, "The shrewmouse will not be good for food. It will prevent the earth plain from looking bare and cheerless."

In this way Raven was busy several days, making birds and fishes and animals. He showed each of them to Man and explained what they were good for. Then Raven flew into the sky, far, far away, and was gone four days. When he came back he brought a salmon to Man.

But Raven noticed that the ponds and lakes were silent and lonely, so he made water bugs to flit upon the surface of the water. He also made the beaver and the muskrat to live around the borders of the ponds. Raven told Man that the beavers would live along the streams and build strong houses, so Man must build a strong house also. Raven said the beavers would be very cunning and only good hunters could catch them. He also told Man how to catch the muskrat and how to use its skin for clothing.

Raven also made flies and mosquitoes and other insects to make the earth plain more cheerful. At first, mosquitoes were like flies ; they did not bite. One day Man killed a deer. After he had cut it up and placed the fat on a bush, he fell asleep. When he awoke he found the mosquitoes had eaten all of it. Then Man was very angry and scolded the mosquitoes. He said, "Never eat meat again. Eat men." Before that mosquitoes never bit people.

When the first baby came on the earth plain, Raven rubbed it all over with white clay. He told Man it would grow into a man like himself. The next morning the baby was a big boy. He ran around pulling up grass and flowers that Raven had planted. By the third day the baby was a full-grown man.

Then another baby was born on the earth plain. She was rubbed over with the white clay. The next day the baby was a big girl, walking around. On the third day she was a full-grown woman.

Now Raven began to be afraid that men would kill all the creatures he had made. He was afraid they would kill them for food and clothing. Therefore Raven went to a creek nearby. He took white clay and shaped it like a bear. Then he waved his wings over it, and the clay became a bear. But Raven jumped very quickly to one side when the bear became alive because it looked fiercely around and growled. Then Raven showed the bear to Man and told him to be careful.

He said the bear was very fierce and would tear him to pieces if he disturbed it.

Then Raven made the seals, and taught Man how to catch them. He also taught Man how to make strong lines from sealskin, and snares for the deer. Then Raven went away to the place of the pea vine.

When he reached the pea vine he found three other men had just fallen from the same pod that Man had fallen from. These men were looking about them in wonder. Raven led them away from the pea vine, but in a different direction from the first man. He brought them close to the sea. Raven stayed with these three men a long time. He taught them how to take wood from the bushes and small trees he planted in hollows and sheltered places, and to make a fire drill, and also a bow. He made many more plants and birds which like the seacoast, but he did not make so many as in the land where Man lived. He taught these men how to make bows and arrows, spears and nets, and how to use them; and also how to capture the seals, which were now plentiful in the sea. Then he taught them how to make kayaks, and how to build houses of drift logs and of bushes, covered with earth. Then he made wives for these men, and went back to Man.

When Raven reached the land where Man lived, he thought the earth plain still looked bare. So, while the others slept, Raven planted birch and spruce and Cottonwood trees to grow in the low places. Then he woke up the people, who were pleased with the trees.

Then Raven taught Man how to make fire with the fire drill, and to place the spark of tinder in a bunch of dry grass and to wave it about until it blazed, and then to put dry wood upon it. He showed them how to roast fish on a stick, and how to make fish traps of splints and willow bark, and how to dry salmon for winter use.

Where Man lived there was now a large village because the people did everything as Raven told them, and therefore all the babies grew up in three days. One day Raven came back and sat down by Man by the creek and they talked of many things. Man asked Raven about the sky-land. Man wanted to see the skyland which Raven had made. Therefore Raven took Man to the land in the sky.

Man found that the skyland was a very beautiful country, and that it had a much better climate than his land. But the people who lived there were very small. Their heads did not reach to Man's hips. The people wore fur clothing, with beautiful patterns, such as people on earth now wear, because Man showed his people how to make them. In the lakes were strange animals which would have killed Man if he had tried to drink of the water. In a dry lake bed, thickly covered with tall grass, Man saw a wonderful animal resting upon the tips of the grasses. It had a long head and six legs. It had fine, thick hair, and on the back of the head were two thick, short horns which bent forward and then curved back at the tips. Raven told Man it took many people to kill this animal.

Then they came to a round hole in the sky and around the edge of the hole was short grass, glowing like fire. Raven said, "This is the star called the moon-dog." Some of the grass had been pulled up. Raven said he had taken some to start the first fire on earth.

Then Raven said to Man, "Shut your eyes. I will take you to another country." Man climbed upon Raven's back and they dropped down through the star hole. They floated a long, long time through the air, then they floated through something else. When they stopped Raven saw he was at the bottom of the sea. Man could breathe there, but it seemed foggy. Raven said that was the appearance of the water. Then Raven said, "I want to make some new animals here; but you must not walk about. You lie down and if you get tired, turn over on the other side."

Man went to sleep lying on one side, and slept a long while. When he waked up, he wanted to turn over, but he could not. Then Man thought, "I wish I could turn over," and at once he turned. As he turned, he was surprised to see that his body was covered with long, white hairs ; and his fingers were long claws. Then he went to sleep again. This he did three times more. Then when he woke up, Raven stood by him. Raven said, "I have changed you into a white bear. How do you like it? "Man could not make a sound until Raven waved his wings over him. Then he said he did not like it; if he was a bear he would have to live on the sea, while his son lived on land; so Man should feel badly. Then Raven struck the white skin with his wings and it fell off. So Man became himself again. But Raven took the empty bearskin, and placed one of his own tail feathers inside it for a spine. Then he waved his wing over it, and a white bear arose. Ever since then white bears have been found on the frozen sea.

Raven said, "How many times did you turn over?"

Man said, "Four."

Raven said, "You slept just four years."

Then Raven made other animals. He made the a-mi-kuk, a large, slimy animal, with thick skin, and with four long, wide-spreading arms. This is a fierce animal and lives in the sea. It wraps its four long arms around a man or a kayak and drags it under the water. A man cannot escape it. If he climbs out of his kayak on the ice, the a-mi-kuk will dart underneath and break the ice. If Man runs away on shore, the a-mi-kuk pursues him by burrowing through the earth. No man can escape from it when once it pursues him.

Then Raven showed Man the walrus, and the dog walrus, with head and teeth like a dog. It always swam with large herds of walrus and with a stroke of its tail could kill a man. He showed him whales and the grampus. Raven told Man that only good hunters could kill a whale, but when one was killed an entire village could feast on it. He showed him also the sea fox, which is so fierce it kills men; and the sea otter, which is like the land otter but has finer fur, tipped with white, and other fishes and animals as they rose to the surface of the water.

Then Raven said, "Close your eyes. Hold fast to me.

Then Man found himself on the shore near his home. The village was very large. His wife was very old and his son was an old man. The people gave him place of honor in the kashim, and made him their headsman. So Man taught the young men many things.

Now Man wanted again to see the skyland, so Raven and

Man went up among the dwarf people and lived there a long time. But on earth the village grew very large; the men killed many animals.

Now in those days, the sun shone always very brightly. No rain ever fell and no winds blew.

Man and Raven were angry because the people killed many animals. They took a long line and a grass basket, one night, and caught ten reindeer which they put into the basket. Now in those days reindeer had sharp teeth, like dogs. The next night Raven took the reindeer and let them down on the earth close to Man's village. Raven said, " Break down the first house you see and kill the people. Men are becoming too many." The reindeer did as Raven commanded. They stamped on the house and broke it down. They ate up the people with their sharp, wolf-like teeth. The next night, Raven let the reindeer down; again they broke down a house and ate up the people with their sharp teeth.

The village people were much frightened. The third night they covered the third house with a mixture of deer fat and berries. On the third night when the reindeer began to tear down the third house, their mouths were filled with the fat and sour berries. Then the reindeer ran away, shaking their heads so violently that all their long, sharp teeth fell out. Ever since then reindeer have had small teeth and cannot harm people.

After the reindeer ran away, Raven and Man returned to the skyland. Man said, " If the people do not stop killing so many animals, they will kill everything you have made. It would be better to take the sun away from them. Then it will be dark and people will die."

Raven said, "That is right. You stay here. I will go and take away the sun."

So Raven went away and took the sun out of the sky. He put it in a skin bag and carried it far away, to a distant part of the skyland. Then it became dark on earth.

The people on earth were frightened when the sun vanished. They offered Raven presents of food and furs if he would bring back the 6un. Raven said, "No." After a while Raven felt sorry for them, so he let them have a little light. He held up the sun in one hand for two days so people could hunt and secure food. Then he put the sun in the skin bag again and the earth was dark. Then, after a long time, when the people made him many gifts, he would let them have a little light again.

Now Raven had a brother living in the village. He was sorry for the earth people. So Raven's brother thought a long time. Then he died. The people put him in a grave box and had a burial feast. Then they left the grave box. At once Raven's brother slipped out of the box and went away from the village. He hid his raven mask and coat in a tree. Soon Raven's wife came for water. When she took up a dipperful to drink, Raven's brother, by magic, became a small leaf. He fell into the water and Raven's wife swallowed him. ....

When Raven-Boy was born he grew very rapidly. He was running about when he was only a few days old. He cried for the sun which was in the skin bag, hanging on the rafters. Raven was fond of the boy so he let him play with the sun; yet he was afraid Raven-Boy would lose the sun, so he watched him. When Raven-Boy began to play out of doors, he cried and begged for the sun. Raven said, "No." Then Raven-Boy cried more than ever. At last Raven gave him the sun in the house. Raven-Boy played with it a long while. When no one was looking, he ran quickly out of the house. He ran to the tree, put on his raven mask and coat, and flew far away with the sun in the skin bag. When Raven-Boy was far up in the sky, he heard Raven call, "Do not hide the sun. Let it out of the bag. Do not keep it always dark." Raven thought the boy had stolen it for himself.

Raven-Boy flew to the place where the sun belonged. He tore off the skin covering and put the sun in its place. Then he saw a broad path leading far away.

He followed it to the side of a hole fringed with short, bright grass. He remembered that Raven had said, "Do not keep it always dark," therefore he made the sky turn, with all the stars and the sun. Thus it is now sometimes dark and sometimes light.

Raven-Boy picked some of the short, bright grass by the edge of the sky hole and stuck it into the sky. This is the morning star.

Raven-Boy went down to the earth. The people were glad to see him. They said, "What has become of Man who went into the skyland with Raven? " Now this was the first time that Raven-Boy had heard of Man. He started to fly up into the sky, but he could get only a small distance above the earth. When he found he could not get back to the sky, Raven-Boy wandered to the second village, where lived the men who had come from the pod of the beach pea. Raven-Boy there married a wife and he had many children. But the children could not fly to the sky. They had lost the magic power. Therefore the ravens now flutter over the tundra like other birds.

CHAPTER THREE
THE TLINGIT CREATION STORY

No one knows just how the story of Raven really begins, so each story starts from the point where the story teller knows. Here it was always begun in this way. Raven was first called Kitkaositiyiqayit, son of Kitkaositiyiqa. When his son was born, Kitkaositiyiqa tried to instruct him and train him in every way and, after he grew up, told him he would give him strength to make a world. After trying in all sorts of ways, Raven finally succeeded. Then there was no light in this world, but it was told him that far up the Nass was a large house in which someone kept light just for himself.

Raven thought over all kinds of plans for getting this light into the world and finally he hit on a good one. The rich man living there had a daughter, and he thought, "I will make myself very small and drop into the water in the form of a small piece of dirt." The girl swallowed this dirt and became pregnant. When her time was completed, they made a hole for her, as was customary, in which she was to bring forth, and lined it with rich furs of all sorts. But the child did not wish to be born on those fine things. Then its grandfather felt sad and said, "What do you think it would be best to put into that hole? Shall we put in moss?" So they put moss inside and the baby was born on it. Its eyes were very bright and moved around rapidly.

Round bundles of varying shapes and sizes hung about on the walls of the house. When the child became a little larger it crawled around back of the people weeping continually, and as it cried it pointed to the bundles. This lasted many days. Then its grandfather said, "Give my grandchild what he is crying for. Give him that one hanging on the end. That is the bag of stars." So the child played with this, rolling it about on the floor back of the people, until suddenly he let it go up through the smoke hole. It went straight up into the sky and the stars scattered out of it, arranging themselves as you now see them. That was what he went there for.

Sometime after this he began crying again, and he cried so much that it was thought he would die. Then his grandfather said, "Untie the next one and give it to him." He played and played with it around behind his mother. After a while he let that go up through the smoke hole also, and there was the big moon.

Now just one thing more remained, the box that held the daylight, and he cried for that. His eyes turned around and showed different colors, and the people began thinking that he must be something other than an ordinary baby. But it always happens that a grandfather loves his grandchild just as he does his own daughter, so the grandfather said, "Untie the last thing and give it to him." His grandfather felt very sad when he gave this to him. When the child had this in his hands, he uttered the raven cry, "Ga," and flew out with it through the smokehole. Then the person from whom he had stolen it said, "That old good for nothing raven has gotten all of my things."

Journeying on, Raven was told of another place, where a man had everlasting spring of water. This man was named Petrel. Raven wanted this water because there was none to drink in this world, but Petrel always slept by his spring, and he had a cover over it so as to keep it all to himself. Then Raven came in and said to him, "My brother-in-law, I have just come to see you. How are you?" He told Petrel of all kinds of things that were happening outside, trying to induce him to go out to look at them, but Petrel was too smart for him and refused.

When night came, Raven said, "I am going to sleep with you, brother-in-law." So they went to bed, and toward morning Raven heard Petrel sleeping very soundly. Then he went outside, took some dog manure and put it around Petrel's buttocks. When it was beginning to grow light, he said, "Wake up, wake up, wake up, brother in-law, you have defecated all over your clothes!" Petrel got up, looked at himself, and thought it was true, so he took his blankets and went outside. Then Raven went over to Petrel's spring, took off the cover and began drinking. After he had drunk up almost all of the water, Petrel came in and saw him. Then Raven flew straight up, crying "Ga."

Before he got through the smoke-hole, however, Petrel said, "My spirits up the smoke hole, catch him." So Raven stuck there, and Petrel put pitchwood on the fire under him so as to make a quantity of smoke. Raven was white before that time, but the smoke made him of the color you find him today. Still he did not drop the water. When the smoke-hole spirits let him go, he flew around the nearest point and rubbed himself all over so as to clear off as much of the soot as possible. This happened somewhere about the Nass, and afterwards he started up this way. First he let some water fall from his mouth and made the Nass. By and by he spit more out and made the Stikine. Next he spit out the Taku River, then the Chilkat, then the Alsek, and all the other large rivers. The small drops that came out of his mouth made the small salmon creeks.

After this Raven went on again and came to a large town where were people who had never seen day light. They were out catching eulachon in the darkness when he came to the bank opposite, and he asked them to take him across but they would not. Then he said to them, "If you don't come over I will have daylight break on you." But they answered, "Where are you from? Do you come from far up the Nass from where the man who has daylight lives?" At this Raven opened his box just a little and shed so great a light on them that they were nearly thrown down. He shut it quickly, but they quarreled with him so much across the creek that he became angry and opened the box completely, when the sun flew up into the sky. Then those people who had sea-otter or fur-seal skins, or the skins of any other sea animals, went into the ocean, while those who had land-otter, bear, or marten skins, or the skins of any other land animals, went into the woods and became the animals whose skins they wore.

Raven went to another place where a crowd of boys were throwing fat at one another. When they hit him with a piece he swallowed it. After a while he took dog's manure and threw at the boys who became scared, ran away, and threw more fat at him. He consumed all in this way, and started on again.

After a while he came to an abandoned camp where lay a piece of jade half buried in the ground, on which some design had been pecked. This he dug up. Far out in the bay he saw a large spring salmon jumping about and wanted to get it but did not know how. Then he stuck his stone into the ground and put eagle down upon the head designed thereon. The next time the salmon jumped, he said, "See here, spring salmon jumping out there, do you know what this green stone is saying to you? It is saying, 'You thing with dirty, filthy back, you thing with dirty, filthy gills, come ashore here.'"

Raven suddenly wanted to defecate and started off. Just then the big spring salmon also started to come ashore, so Raven said, "Just wait, my friend, don't come ashore yet for I have some business to attend to." So the salmon went out again. Afterward Raven took a piece of wild celery, and, when the salmon did come ashore, he struck it with this and killed it. Because Raven made this jade talk to the salmon, people have since made stone axes, picks, and spears out of it.

Then Raven, carrying along the spring salmon, got all kinds of birds, little and big, as his servants. When he came to a good place to cook his fish he said to all of them, "Here, you young fellows, go after skunk cabbage. We will bury this in the ground and roast it." After they had brought it down, however, he said, "I don't want any of that. My wife has defecated all over that, and I will not use it. Go back and pass over two mountains." While they were gone, Raven put all of the salmon except one fat piece cut from around the navel which is usually cooked separately, into the skunk cabbage and buried it in the fire. Before they returned, he dug this up and ate it, after which he put the bones back into the fire and covered them up.

When the birds at last came back he said to them, "I have been across two mountains myself. Now it is time to dig it up. Dig it out." Then all crowded around the fire and dug, but, when they got it up, there was nothing there but bones.

By and by the birds dressed one another in different ways so that they might be named from their dress. They tied the hair of the blue jay up high with a string, and they added a long tail to another crested bird called the Tsegeni. Then they named one another. Raven let out the Tsegeni and told him that when the salmon comes he must call its slime unclean and stay high up until the salmon are all gone.

Now Raven started off with the piece of salmon belly and came to a place where Bear and his wife lived. He entered and said, "My aunt's son, is this you?" The piece of salmon he had buried behind a little point. Then Bear told him to sit down and said, "I will roast some dry salmon for you." So he began to roast it. After it was done, he set a dish close to the fire and slit the back of his hands with a knife so as to let grease run out for Raven to eat on his salmon. After he had fixed the salmon, he cut a piece of flesh out from in front of his thighs and put it into the dish. That is why bears are not fat in that place.

Now Raven wanted to give a dinner to Bear in return, so he, too, took out a piece of fish, roasted it, set out the dish Bear had used, dose to the fire and slit up the back of his hand, thinking that grease would run out of it. But instead nothing but white bubbles came forth. Although he knew he could not do it, he tried in every way.

Then Raven asked Bear, "Do you know of any halibut fishing ground out here?" He said "No." Raven said, "Why! What is the use of staying here by this salt water, if you do not know of any fishing ground? I know a good fishing ground right out here called Just on-the-edge-of-kelp. There are always halibut swimming there, mouth up, ready for the hook."

By and by Raven got the piece of fish he had hidden behind the point and went out to the bank in company with Bear and Cormorant. Cormorant sat in the bow, Bear in the middle, and, because he knew where the fishing ground was, Raven steered. When they arrived Raven stopped the canoe all at once. He said to them, "Do you see that mountain? When you see that mountain, that is where you want to fish." After this, Raven began to fill the canoe with halibut. So Bear asked him, "What do you use for bait anyhow, my friend?" Raven answered, "I'll use the skin covering the testicles as bait." The bear asked, "Is it alright to use mine?" But the raven said, "I don't want to do it, for they might be too wasted." Soon the bear was urging it strongly, "Cut them off!" So the Raven, sharpening a short knife, said, "Place them on the seat." Then the Raven cut them off, so that the Bear, crying out, fell from the boat and, dying, spilled into the waves with one last sigh.

After a while Raven said to Cormorant, "There is a louse coming down on the side of your head. Come here. Let me take it off." When he came close to him, he picked it off. Then he said, "Open your mouth so that I can put it on your tongue." When he did open his mouth, however, Raven reached far back and pulled his tongue out. He did this because he did not want Cormorant to tell about what he had done. He told Cormorant to speak, but Cormorant made only a gabbling noise. "That is how young fellows ought to speak," said Raven. Then Raven towed the dead body of the bear behind the point and carried it ashore there. Afterwards he went to Bear's wife and began to take out his halibut. He said to the female bear, "My father's sister, cut out all the stomachs of the halibut and roast them." So she went down on the beach to cut them out. While she was working on the rest of the halibut, he cooked the stomachs and filled them with hot rocks. Then he went down and said to her, "You better come up. I have cooked all those stomachs for you. You better wash your hands, come up, and eat." After that the Cormorant came in and tried to tell what had happened but made only a gabbling sound. Raven said to the bear, "Do you know what that fellow is talking about? He is saying that there were lots of halibut out where we fished. Every time we tried to get a canoe load they almost turned us over." When she was about to eat he said, "People never chew what I get. They always swallow it whole." Before she began she asked Raven where her husband was, and Raven said, "Somehow or other he caught nothing, so we landed him behind the point. He is cutting alders to make alder hooks. He is sitting there yet."

After the bear had swallowed all of the food she began to feel uneasy in her stomach, and Raven said to Cormorant, "Run outside quickly and get her some water." Then she drank a great quantity of water, and the things in her stomach began to boil harder and harder. Said Raven, "Run out Cormorant." He did so, and Raven ran after him. Then the female bear ran about inside the house grabbing at everything and finally fell dead. Then Raven skinned the female bear, after which he went around the point and did the same thing to the male. While he was busy there Cormorant came near him, but he said, "Keep away, you small Cormorant," and struck him on the buttocks with his hand saying, "Go out and stay on those rocks." Ever since then the cormorants have been there. Raven stayed in that place until he had consumed both of the bears.

Starting on again, Raven came to a place where many people were encamped fishing. They used nothing but fat for bait. He entered a house and asked what they used for bait. They said "Fat." Then he said, "Let me see you put enough on your hooks for bait," and he noticed carefully how they baited and handled their hooks. The next time they went out, he walked off behind a point and went under water to get this bait. Now they got bites and pulled up quickly, but there was nothing on their hooks. This continued for a long time. The next time they went out they felt the thing again, but one man among them who knew just how fish bite, jerked at the right moment and felt that he had caught something. The line went around in the water very fast. They pulled away, however, until they got Raven under the canoe, and he kicked against it very hard. All at once his nose came out, and they pulled it up. When they landed, they took it to the chief's house and said, "We have caught a wonderful thing. It must be the nose of the

Gonaqadet." So they took it, put eagle down on it, and hung it up on the wall.

After that, Raven came ashore at the place where he had been in the habit of going down, got a lot of spruce gum and made a new nose out of it. Then he drew a root hat down over his face and went to the town. Beginning at the nearer end he went through the houses saying "I wonder in what house are the people who caught that Gonaqadet's nose." After he had gone halfway, he entered the chief's house and inquired, "Do you know where are the people who caught that Gonaqadet's nose?" They answered, "There it is on the wall." Then he said, "Bring it here. Let me examine it." So they gave it to him. "This is great," he said, and he put up his hat to examine it. "Why," said he, "this house is dark. You ought to take off the smoke-hole cover. Let someone run up and take it off so that I can see." But, as soon as they removed it, he put the nose in its place, cried "Ga," and flew away. They did not find out who he was.

Going thence, Raven saw a number of deer walking around on the beach, with a great deal of fat hanging out through their noses. As he passed one of these, he said, "Brother, you better blow your nose. Lots of dirt is hanging out of it." When the deer would not do this, Raven came close to him, wiped his nose and threw the fat by his own side. Calling out, "Just for the Raven," he swallowed it.

Now Raven formed a certain plan. He got a small canoe and began paddling along the beach saying, "I wonder who is able to go along with me." Mink came down and said, "How am I?" and Raven said, "What can you do?" Said Mink, "When I go to camp with my friends, I make a bad smell in their noses. That's what I can do." But Raven said, "I guess not. You might make a hole in my canoe," so he went along farther. The various animals and birds would come down and say, "How am I?" but he did not even listen. After some time Deer ran down to him, saying, "How am I?" Then he answered, "Come this way, come this way." Finally Raven came ashore and said to the Deer, "Don't hurt yourself." By and by Raven said "Not very far from here my father has been making a canoe. Let us go there and look at it."

Then Raven brought him to a large valley. He took very many pieces of dried wild celery and laid them across the valley, covering them with moss. Said Raven, watch me, watch me." Repeating this over and over he went straight across on it, for he is light. Afterwards he said to the Deer, "Now you come and try it. It will not break," and he crossed once more. "You better try it now," he said. "Come on over." Deer did so, but, as he was on the way, he broke through the bridge and smashed his head to pieces at the bottom. Then Raven went down, walked all over him, and said to himself, "I wonder where I better start, at the root of his tail, at the eyes, or at the heart." Finally he began at his anus, skinning as he went along. He ate very fast.

When he started on from this place, he began crying. The fowls asked him, "What has become of your friend?"

"Someone has taken him and pounded him on the rocks, and I have been walking around and hopping around since he died."

By and by he came to a certain cliff and saw a door in it swing open. He got behind a point quickly, for he knew that here lived the woman who has charge of the falling and rising of the tide. Far out Raven saw some kelp, and, going out to this, he climbed down on it to the bottom of the sea and gathered up a number of small sea urchins which were lying about there. He brought these ashore and began eating, making a great gulping noise as he did so. Meanwhile the woman inside of the cliff kept mocking him saying, "During what tide did he get those things?"

While Raven was eating, the Mink came along, and Raven said, "Come here. Come here."

Then he went on eating. And the woman again said, "On what tide did you get those sea urchins you are making so much noise about?"

"That is not your business," answered Raven. "Keep quiet or I will stick them all over your buttocks." Finally Raven became angry, seized the knife he was cutting up the sea urchins with and slit up the front of the cliff out of which she spoke. Then he ran in, knocked her down and began sticking the spines into her buttocks.

"Stop, Raven, stop," she cried, "The tide will begin to go down."

So he said to his, servant, Mink, "Run outside and see how far down the tide has gone."

Mink ran out and said, "It is just beginning to go down." The next time he came in he said, "The tide is still farther down." The third time he said, "The tide is lower yet. It has uncovered everything on the beach."

Then Raven said to the old woman, "Are you going to let the tide rise and fall again regularly through the months and years?" She answered "Yes."

Because Raven did this while he was making the world, nowadays, when a woman gets old and cannot do much more work, there are spots all over her buttocks.

After the tide had gone down very far he and his servant went out. He said to Mink, "The thing that will be your food from now on is the sea urchin. You will live on it." The tide now goes up and down because he treated this woman so.

Now Raven started on from this place crying, "My wife, my wife! " Coming to some trees, he saw a lot of gum on one of them and said to it, "Why! You are just like me. You are in the same state." For he thought the tree was crying.

After this he got a canoe and began paddling along. By and by Petrel met him in another canoe. So he brought his canoe alongside and said, "Is this you, my brother-in-law? Where are you from?"

He answered, "I am from over there."

Then Raven began to question him about the events in this world, asking him how long ago they happened, etc. He said, "When were you born? How long have you been living?"

And Petrel answered, "I have been living ever since the great liver came up from under the earth. I have been living that long." So said Petrel.

"Why! That is but a few minutes ago," said Raven.

Then Petrel began to get angry and said to Raven, "When were you born?"

"I was born before this world was known." Said the Raven

"That is just a little while back." Replied the Petrel

They talked back and forth until they became very angry. Then Petrel pushed Raven's canoe away from him and put on his hat called fog-hat so that Raven could not see where he was. The world was round for him in the fog. At last he shouted, "My brother-in-law, Petrel, you are older than I am. You have lived longer than I."

Petrel also took water from the sea and sprinkled it in the air so that it fell through the fog as very fine rain. Said Raven, "Ayee! Ayee!" He did not like it at all. After Petrel had fooled him for some time, he took off Fog-hat and found Raven close beside him, pulling about in all directions. Then Raven said to Petrel, "Brother-in-law, you better let that hat go into this world." So he let it go. That is why we always know, when we see fog coming out of an open space in the woods and going right back again, that there will be good weather.

Leaving this place, Raven came to another where he saw something floating not far from shore, though it never came any nearer. He assembled all kinds of fowl. Toward evening he looked at the object and saw that it resembled fire. So he told a chicken hawk which had a very long bill to fly out to it, saying, "Be very brave. If you get some of that fire, do not let go of it." The chicken hawk reached the place, seized some fire and started back as fast as it could fly, but by the time it got the fire to Raven its bill was burned off. That is why its bill is short. Then Raven took some red cedar, and some white stones which are found on the beach, and he put fire into them so that it could be found ever afterward all over the world.

After he had finished distributing the fire he started on again and came to a town where there were many people.

He saw what looked like a large animal far off on the ocean with fowl all over the top of it. He wondered very much what it was and at last thought of a way of finding out. He said to one of his friends, "Go up and cut a cane for me." Then he carved this cane so as to resemble two tentacles of a devil fish. He said, "No matter how far off a thing is, this cane will always reach it."

Afterward he went to the middle of the town and said, "I am going to give a feast. My mother is dead, and I am going to beat the drums this evening. I want all of the people to come in and see me."

In the evening he assembled all of the people, and they began to beat drums. Then he held the cane in his hands and moved it around horizontally, testing it. He kept saying "Up, up, up" He said, "I have never given any feast for my mother, and it is time I did it, but I have nothing with which to give a feast. Therefore I made this cane, and I am going to give a feast for my mother with this wonderful thing."

Then he got the people all down on the beach and extended his cane toward the mysterious object until it reached it. And he began to draw it in little by little, saying to the people, "Sing stronger all the time." When it struck land, a wave burst it open. It was an everlasting house, containing everything that was to be in the waters of the world. He told the people to carry up fish and they did so. If one had a canoe, he filled it; if he had a box, he filled that; and those that had canoes also boiled eulachon in them. Since then they have known how to boil them. With all of these things Raven gave the feast for his mother.

After this was over he thought up a plot against the killer whales and sent an invitation to them. Then he told each of his people to make a cane that would reach very much above his head. So, when the killer whales came in and inquired, "What do the people use those canes for that extend up over their heads?" he replied, "They stick them down into their heads." They asked him several times, and he replied each time in the same way.

After a while one of the whales said, "Suppose we try it."

Raven was glad to hear that and said, "All right, we will try it with you people, but the people I have invited must not look when I put a cane into anyone's head."

Then he went away and whittled a number of sticks until they were very sharp. After that he laid all of the killer whales on the beach at short distances apart, and again he told them not to look up while he was showing one how it was done. Then he took a hammer and drove his sticks into the necks of these whales one after the other so that they died. But the last one happened to look up, saw what was being done, and jumped into the ocean.

Now Raven and another person started to boil out the killer whales' grease, and the other man had more than he. So Raven dreamed a dream which informed him that a lot of people were coming to fight with him, and, when such people really did make their appearance, he told his companion to run out. After he had done so, Raven quickly drank all the latter's grease. By and by, however, the man returned, threw Raven into a grease box, and shut him in, and started to tie it up with a strong rope. Then Raven called out, "My brother, do not tie the box up very strongly. Tie it with a piece of straw such as our forefathers used to use." The man did so, after which he took the box up on a high cliff and kicked it over.

Then Raven, breaking the straw, flew out, crying "Ga."

When he got to the other side of the point, he alighted and began wiping himself.

Next he came to a large whale blowing along out at sea, and noticed that every time it came up, its mouth was wide open. Then Raven took a knife and something with which to make fire. When the whale came up again he flew into its mouth and sat down at the farther end of its stomach. Near the place where he had entered he saw something that looked like an old woman. It was the whale's uvula. When the whale came up, it made a big noise, the uvula went to one side and the herring and other fish it lived on poured right in. Then Raven began eating all these things that the whale had swallowed, and presently, he made a fire to cook the fat of the whale itself that hung inside. Last of all he ate the heart

As soon as he cut this out, the whale threw itself about in the water and soon floated up dead. Raven felt this and said, "I wish it would float up on a good sandy beach." After he had wished this many times, the whale began to drift along, and it finally floated ashore on a long sandy beach.

After a while some young fellows who were always shooting about in this neighborhood with their bows and arrows, heard a voice on the beach say, "I wonder who will make a hole on the top so that he can be my friend."

The boys ran home to the town and reported, "We heard a queer noise. Something floated ashore not far from this place, and a person inside said, 'I wish that somebody would make a hole above me so that he can be my friend.'"

Then the people assembled around the whale and heard Raven's words very clearly. They began to cut a hole just over the place these came from and presently they heard someone inside say, "Xone'e." When the hole was large enough, Raven flew straight up out of it until he was lost to sight. And they said to him, "Fly to any place where you would like to go."

After that they cut the whale up and in course of time came to the spot where Raven had lighted his fire to make oil.

Meanwhile Raven flew back of their camp to a large dead tree that had crumbled into fine pieces and began rubbing on it to dry himself. When he thought that the people were through making oil, he dressed himself up well and repaired to the town. There he said to the people, "Was anything heard in that whale?" and one answered, "Yes, a queer noise was heard inside of the whale."

"I wonder what it was," said Raven.

After their food was prepared, Raven said to the people, "Long ago, when a sound was heard inside of a whale, all the people moved out of their town so as not to be killed. All who remained were destroyed. So you better move from this town."

Then all of the people said, "All of us better move from this town rather than be destroyed." So they went off leaving all of their things, and Raven promptly took possession of them.

Raven once went to a certain place outside of here (Sitka) in his canoe. It was calm there, but he began rocking the canoe up and down with his feet until he had made a great many waves. Therefore, there are many waves there now even when it is calm outside, and a canoe going in thither always gets lost.

By and by Raven came to a seagull standing at the mouth of a creek and said to it, "What are you sitting in this way for? How do you call your new month?" "Yadaqol," replied the seagull. Raven was questioning him in this way because he saw many herring out at sea. So he said, "I don't believe at all what you say. Fly out and see if you can bring in a herring." This is why, until the present time, people have differed in their opinions concerning the months and have disputed with one another.

After they had quarreled over it for a long time, the gull became angry, flew out to sea, and brought back a big herring. He landed near Raven and laid the herring beside him, but, when Raven tried to get it, he gulped it down.

In another direction from the seagull Raven saw a large heron and went over to it. He said to the heron, " Hey, the Seagull is calling you Big-long-legs-always-walking-upon-the beach."

Then, although the heron did not reply, he went back to the sea gull and said, "Do you know what that heron is saying about you? He says that you have a big stomach and get your red eyes by sitting on the beach always looking out on the ocean for something to eat."

Then he went back to the heron and said to it, "When I meet a man of my own size, I always kick him just below the stomach. That fellow is talking too much about you. Go over, and I will help you thrash him."

So the heron went over toward the seagull, and, when he came close to it, Raven said, "Kick him just under his stomach." He did so, and the big herring came out. Then Raven swallowed it quickly saying, "Just for the Raven."

Going on again, Raven came to a canoe in which were some people lying asleep along with a big salmon which he took away. When the people awoke, they saw the trail where he had dragged it off, and they followed him. They found him lying asleep by the fire after having eaten the salmon. Seeing his gizzard hanging out at his buttocks, they twisted it off, ran home with it and used it as a shiny ball; this is why no human being now has a gizzard.

The people knew it was Raven's gizzard, so they liked to show it about, and they knocked it around so much that it grew large by the accumulation of sand. But Raven did not like losing his gizzard. He was cold without it and had to get close to the fire. When he came to the place where they were playing with it, he said, "Let it come this way." No sooner had they gotten it near him, however, than they knocked it away again. After a while it reached him, and he seized it and ran off, with all the boys after him. As he ran he washed it in water and tried to fit it back in place. It was too hot from much knocking about, and he had to remove it again. He washed it again but did not get all of the sand off. That is why the raven's gizzard is big and looks as if it had not been washed.

Next Raven came to a town where a man called Fog-on-the-Salmon lived. He wanted to marry this man's daughter because he always had plenty of salmon. He had charge of that place. So he married her, and they dried quantities of salmon, after which they filled many animal stomachs with salmon eggs. Then he loaded his canoe and started home. He put all of the fish eggs into the bow. On the way it became stormy, and they could not make much headway, so he became tired and threw his paddles into the bow, exclaiming to his wife, "Now you paddle!"
Then the salmon eggs shouted out, "It is very hard to be in stomachs. Hand the paddles here and let me pull." So the

salmon eggs did, and, when they reached home, Raven took all of them and dumped them over board. But the dried salmon he carried up. That is why people now use dried salmon and do not care much for salmon eggs.

Journeying on, Raven came to a seal sitting on the edge of a rock, and he wanted to get it, but the seal jumped into the ocean. Then he said, "Yakoctal," because he was so sorry about it. Farther on he came to a town and went behind it to watch. After a while a man came out, took a little club from a certain place where he kept it in concealment, and said to it, "My little club, do you see that seal out there? Go and get it." So it went out and brought the little seal ashore. The club was hanging to its neck. Then the man took it up and said, "My little club, you have done well," after which he put it back in its place and returned to the town. Raven saw where it was kept, but first he went to the town and spoke kindly to the owner of it.

In the night, however, when everyone was asleep, he went back to the club, carried it behind a point and said to it, "See here, my little club, you see that seal out in the water. Go and get it." But the club would not go because it did not know him. After he had tried to get it to go for some time, he became angry and said to it, "Little club, don't you see that seal out there?" He kept striking it against a rock until he broke it in pieces.

Coming to a large bay, Raven talked to it in order to make it into Nass (i. e., he wanted to make it just like the Nass), but, when the tide was out great numbers of dams on the flats made so much noise shooting up at him that his voice was drowned, and he could not succeed. He tried to put all kinds of berries there but in vain. After many attempts, he gave it up and went away saying, "I tried to make you into Nass, but you would not let me. So you can be called

Skana'x" (the name of a place to the southward of Sitka).

Two brothers started to cross the Stikine River, but Raven saw them and said, "Be stones there." So they became stones.

Starting on, he came to the ground-hog people on the mainland. His mother had died some time before this, and, as he had no provisions with which to give a feast, he came to the ground hogs to get some. The ground-hog people know when slides descend from the mountains, and they know that spring is then near at hand, so they throw all of their winter food out of their burrows. Raven wanted them to do this, so he said, "There is going to be a world snow slide." But the ground-hog chief answered, "Well! Nobody in this town knows about it."

Toward spring, however, the slide really took place, and the ground hogs then threw all of their green herbs, roots, etc., outside to him.

After this he said to the people, "Make ear pendants because I am going to invite the whole world." He was going to invite everyone because he had heard that the Gonaqadet had a Chilkat blanket and a hat, and he wanted to see them. First he invited the Gonaqadet and afterwards the other chiefs of all the tribes in the world. At the appointed time they began to come in. When the Gonaqadet came in he had on his hat with many crowns and his blanket but was surrounded by a fog. Inside of the house, however, he appeared in his true form. It is from this feast of Raven's that people now like to attend feasts. It is also from this that, when a man is going to have a feast, he has a many-crowned hat carved on top of the dead man's grave post.

Raven made a woman under the earth to have charge of the rise and fall of the tides. One time he wanted to learn about everything under the ocean and had this woman raise the water so that he could go there. He had it rise very slowly so that the people had time to load their canoes and get into them. When the tide had lifted them up between the mountains they could see bears and other wild animals walking around on the still exposed tops. Many of the bears swam out to them, and at that time those who had their dogs had good protection. Some people walled the tops of the mountains about and tied their canoes inside. They could not take much wood up with them. Sometimes hunters see the rocks they piled up there, and at such times it begins to grow foggy. That was a very dangerous time. The people who survived could see trees swept up roots and all by the rush of waters and large devilfish and other creatures were carried up by it.

When the tide began to fall, all the people followed it down, but the trees were gone and they had nothing to use as firewood, so they were destroyed by the cold. When Raven came back from under the earth, if he saw a fish left on top of a mountain or in a creek, he said, "Stay right there and become a stone." So it became a stone. If he saw any person coming down, he would say, "Turn to a stone just where you are," and it did so.

After that the sea went down so far that it was dry everywhere. Then Raven went about picking up the smallest fish, as bull heads and tom cod, which he strung on a stick, while a friend who was with him at this time, named Cakaku, took large creatures like whales. With the grease he boiled out, Cakaku filled an entire house, while Raven filled only a small bladder.

Raven stayed with Cakaku and one night had a dream. He

said to his friend, "I dreamed that a great enemy came and attacked us." Then he had all the fowls assemble and come to fight, so that his dream might be fulfilled. As soon as Raven had told his dream, Cakaku went down and saw the birds. Then Raven went into the house and began drinking up his grease. But the man came back, saw what Raven was doing, and threw him into a grease box, which he started to tie up with a strong rope. Raven, however, called out, "My brother, do not tie me up with a strong rope, but take a straw such as our forefathers used to employ." He did so. Then Raven drank up all the grease in the box, and, when the man took him up on a high cliff and kicked him off, he came out easily and flew away crying "Ga."

One time Raven assembled all the birds in preparation for a feast and had the bears in the rear of his house as guests. All the birds had canes and helped him sing. As he sang along Raven would say quietly, "Do you think one of you could fly into the anus of a bear?" Then he would start another song and end it by saying in much the same language, "One of you ought to fly up into that hole." He kept taunting the birds with their inability to do this, so, when the bears started out, the wren, "bird-that can-go-through-a-hole") flew up into the anus of one of them and came out with his intestines. Before it had pulled them far out the bear fell dead. Then Raven chased all of the small birds away, sat down, and began eating. Raven never got full because he had eaten the black spots off of his own toes. He learned about this after having inquired everywhere for some way of bringing such a state about. Then he wandered through all around the world in search of things to eat.

After all the human beings had been destroyed Raven made new ones out of leaves. Because he made this new generation, people know that he must have changed all of the first people who had survived the flood into stones. Since human beings were made from leaves, people always die off rapidly in the fall of the year when flowers and leaves are falling.

At the time when he made this world, Raven made a devilfish digging-stick and went around to all created things saying, "Are you going to hurt human beings ? Say now either yes or no." Those that said "No" he passed by; those that said "Yes" he rooted up. He said to the people, "When the tide goes out, your food will be there. When the tide comes in, your food will be in the woods," indicating bear and other forest animals.

In Raven's time the butts of ferns were already cooked, but, after some women had brought several of these in, Raven broke a stick over the fern roots. Therefore they became green like this stick. He also broke the roots up into many layers one above another.

Devilfish were very fat then, and the people used to make grease out of them, but, when Raven came to a place where they were making he said, "Give me a piece of that hard thing." That is why its fatness left it.

One time Raven invited all the tribes of little people and laid down bear skins for them to sit on. After they had come in and reached the bear skins, they shouted to one another, "Here is a swampy, open space." That was the name they gave to those places on the skins from which the hair had fallen out. By and by Raven seized the bear skins and shook them over the fire, when all the little people flew into the eyes of the human beings. He said, "You shall be pupils in people's eyes," and ever since human beings have had them.

Now he went on from this place and camped by himself. There he saw a large sculpin trying to get ashore below him, and he said to it, "My uncle's son, come ashore here. Come way up. One time, when you and I were going along in our uncle's canoe we fell into the water. So come up a little farther."

Raven was very hungry, and, when the Sculpin came ashore, he seized it by its big, broad tail intending to eat it. But it slipped through his fingers. This happened many times, and each time the Sculpin's tail became smaller. That is why it is so slender today. Then Raven said to it, From now on, you shall be named Sculpin.'"

Raven had a blanket which kept blowing out from him, so he threw it into the water and let it float away. Then he obtained a wife, and, as he was traveling along with her, he said, "There is going to be a great southwest wind. We better stop here for a little, wife. I expect my blanket ashore here." After a while it came in. Then his wife said to him, "Take your blanket ashore and throw it on some branches.

He did so and it became stink currant. When they went on farther the sea became so rough that his wife was frightened and told him to put ashore some of the fat with which his canoe was loaded. He did this, but was so angry with his wife for having asked him, that he said to her, "You better put ashore your sewing basket," and so she did.

Then he left his wife and went along by himself. He assembled very many young birds, and, when he camped he told them to go after some drinking water.

Afterwards he came to a certain place and started to make a salmon creek. He said, "This woman shall be at the head of this creek." The woman he spoke of had long teats, so he

41

called her Woman-with long-teats-floating-around, saying, "When the salmon come to the creeks, they shall all go up to see her." That is why salmon run up the creeks.

After this he went into the woods and set out to make the porcupine. For quills he took pieces of yellow cedar bark, which he set all the way up and down its back so that bears would be afraid of it. This is why bears never eat porcupines. He said to the porcupine, "Whenever anyone comes near you, throw your tail about." This is why people are afraid of it when it does so.

Now Raven went off to a certain place and made the west wind. He said to it, "You shall be my son's daughter. No matter how hard you blow you shall hurt nobody.

He took up a piece of red salmon and said to it, "If anyone is not strong enough to paddle home he shall take up this fish and blow behind him."

Raven is a grandchild of the mouse . That is why a mouse can never get enough to eat.

Raven also made the south wind. When the south wind climbs on top of a rock it never ceases to blow.

He made the north wind, and on top of a mountain he made a house for it with something like ice hanging down on the sides. Then he went in and said to it, "Your buttocks are white." This is why the mountains are white with snow.

He made all the different races, as the Haida and the Tsimshian. They are human beings like the Tlingit, but he made their languages different.

He also made the dog. It was at first a human being and did

everything Raven wanted done, but he was too quick with everything, so Raven took him by the neck and pushed him down, saying, "You are nothing but a dog. You shall have four legs."

One time Raven came to a certain thing called fat-on-the-sea, which stuck out of the ocean. He kept saying to it, "Get down a little," so it kept going under the surface. But every time it came up he took his paddle and cut part off. It did this seven times, but, when he spoke to it the eighth time, it went down out of sight, and he never saw it again.

As he was traveling along in another place, a wild celery came out, became angry with Raven, and said, "You are always wandering around for things to eat." Then he named it wild celery and said to it, "You shall stay there, and people shall eat you.

Once he passed a large tree and saw something up in it called Caxda'q . Raven called out "Caxda'q," and it shouted back, "You Raven." They called back and forth to each other for some time.

CHAPTER FOUR
THE HAIDA CREATION STORY

After the great flood had at long last receded, Raven had gorged himself on the delicacies left by the receding water, so for once, perhaps the first time in his life, he wasn't hungry. but his other appetites, his curiosity and the unquenchable itch to meddle and provoke things, to play tricks on the world and its creatures, these remained unsatisfied.

Raven gazed up and down the beach. It was pretty, but lifeless. There was no one about to upset, or play tricks upon. Raven sighed. He crossed his wings behind him and strutted up and down the sand, his shiny head cocked, his sharp eyes and ears alert for any unusual sight or sound. The mountains and sea, the sky now ablaze with the sun by day and the moon and stars he had placed there, it was all pretty, but lifeless. Finally Raven cried out to the empty sky with a loud exasperated cry.

And before the echoes of his cry faded from the shore, he heard a muffled squeak. He looked up and down the beach for its source and saw nothing. He strutted back and and forth, once, twice, three times and still saw nothing. Then he spied a flash of white in the sand.

There, half buried in the sand was a giant clamshell. As his shadow fell upon it, he heard another muffled squeak. Peering down into the opening between the halves of the shell, he saw it was full of tiny creatures, cowering in fear at his shadow.

Raven was delighted. Here was a break in the monotony of the day. But how was he to get the creatures to come out of their shell and play with him? Nothing would happen as long as they stayed inside the giant clamshell.

They were not going to come out as long as they were so afraid of him. So Raven leaned over his head, close to the shell, and with all the cunning and skill of that smooth trickster's tongue, that had so often gotten him in and out of so many misadventures during his troubled and troublesome existence, he coaxed and cajoled and coerced the little creatures to come out and play in his wonderful shiny new world.

As you know the Raven has two voices, one harsh and strident, and the other which he used now, a seductive, bell-like croon which seems to come from the depth of the sea, or out of the cave where winds are born. It is an irresistible sound, one of the loveliest in the world.

It wasn't long before first one and then another of the little shell-dwellers emerged from the shell. Some scurried back when they saw the Raven, but eventually curiosity overcame their caution and all of them had crept or scrambled out.

Very strange creatures they were: two legged like Raven, but otherwise very different. They had no feathers. Nor fur. They had no great beak. Their skin was pale, and they were naked except for the dark hair upon round, flat-featured heads. Instead of strong wings like raven, they had think stick-like arms that waved and fluttered constantly. They were the first humans.

For a long time Raven amused himself with these new playthings. Laughing as they explored with wonder a much expanded world. Sometimes they helped each other, sometimes they fought over something they had found.

Raven even taught them some tricks, but soon he became tired of their ceaseless activity.

For one thing, they were so helpless out in the world. They needed shelter from the sun and the rain. They were so fearful and seemed so small. And there were no girls among them, only boys. Raven was about to shove these tired, demanding and annoying creatures back into their shell and forget them, when, as so often happens with Raven, he had an idea for some fun.

Raven began to search for the girls. For it is the way of things in the world that there are both males and females of every creature. Somewhere there must be girls. Raven searched and searched. Under logs and behind rocks, he looked. But he could not find the hiding place of the first girls.

But as he searched, the tide was going out, and as it reached its lowest, the Raven spotted some giant Chitons clinging to the rocks. These giant shell fish had but one shell, fastened tightly to the rocks with huge soft lips around their edges. Raven pried one loose with his beak. And there inside was a girl. He pried off another, and another, and another in each was a girl. They were very similar to the creatures he had found in the clamshell, but more like the Chiton, softer and rounder, in contrast to the hard shell and strong muscles of the clam. And these were just as frightened of the Raven. He gathered them onto his back with difficulty, and brought them to the boys he had found in the clamshell.

Raven was expecting the boy creatures to be very happy he had found the girl creatures, but to his surprise. They were frightened of them and some even ran back into the Giant clamshell to hide. The girl creatures were just as shy and huddled together watching the males with fearful and curious eyes. Both the boy and girl creatures seemed very modest and sought to cover their bodies with strips of kelp and woven sea weed from the shore.

The boy creatures were astonished and embarrassed and confused by feelings they had never before had. They didn't know how to behave. But some of them overcame their fear and began to do things to attract the attention of the girl creatures Raven had brought. Some began to show off the tricks they had been taught - leaping and running and wrestling with other boy creatures. Some of the girl creatures overcame their shyness, first with quick glances then finally allowing the boy creatures to approach them, and even leaving the safety of their huddled group of girl creatures. Gradually the two groups began to mingle into one and just as gradually the boy creatures and girl creatures overcame all their fears and paired off, walking hand in hand, their eyes absorbed in each other totally.

Raven watched all this with increasing interest and surprise. Among all the creatures of the world, there were few whose males and females were so very different. The males proud, agile and strong, the females gentle, soft and tender. Sometimes the males would be too rough in their play with the females and there would be tears. But those same tears seemed to have an emotional power over the males bringing out of them protective instincts. The strengths of each balanced the weakness of each.

And since that day, Raven has never been bored. In fact, at times he has almost regretted bringing the first men and women together. From the strong muscles of the clam and the soft lips of the Chiton, from the pairing of these first people came the first families. Children were born, some strong and male, some soft and female. Many generations have been born, have grown and flourished, have built and created or fought and destroyed. Many have blamed the Raven for playing a terrible joke on humanity, for often men and women just barely get along, but somehow from this strange combination of reason and intuition, of muscle and emotion arose that which was needed for the race to survive the storms of life on the shores.

Raven himself felt strange protective urges for these first people. Though a glutton and trickster by nature, he would again and again provide for these creatures he found in the clamshell. In time he would bring them the Sun, Moon and Stars; Fire; Salmon and Cedar, teach them the secrets of hunting, and the world. Raven would watch these weak creatures become both strong and loving, courageous and compassionate, able to fend for themselves and survive.

And their children were no timid shell-dwellers, but they continued to be children of the wild coast, of the stormy shores between the land and the sea. They challenged the strength of the stormy north Pacific wresting their livelihoods from the sea even as they made their homes on its shores.

CHAPTER FIVE
THE BRINGING OF THE LIGHT BY THE RAVEN

Inuit

In the first days, the sun and moon were in the sky. Then the sun and moon were taken away and people had only the light of the stars. Even the magic of the shamans failed to bring back the light.

Now there was an orphan boy in the village who sat with the humble people over the entrance way of the kashim. He was despised by everyone. When the magic of the shamans failed to bring back the sun and moon into the sky the boy mocked them. He said, "What fine shamans you must be. You cannot bring back the light, but I can." Then the shamans were angry and beat that boy and drove him out of the kashim. Now this boy was like any other boy until he put on a raven coat he had. Then he became Raven.

Now the boy went to his aunt's house. He told her the shamans had failed to bring back the light, and they had beaten him when he mocked them. The boy said, "Where are the sun and moon?"

The aunt said, "I do not know."

The boy said, "I am sure you know. Look what a finely sewed coat you wear. You could not sew it that way if you did not know where the light is."

Thus they argued.

Then the aunt said, "If you wish to find the light, go far to the south. Go on snowshoes. You will know the place when you get there."

The boy put on his snowshoes and set off toward the south. Many days he travelled and the darkness was always the same. When he had gone a very long way he saw far in front of him a ray of light. Then the boy hurried on. As he went farther the light showed again, plainer than before. Then it vanished for a time. Thus it kept appearing and vanishing.

At last the boy came to a large hill. One side was brightly lighted; the other side was black as night. Close to the hill was a hut. A man was shoveling snow from in front of it. The man tossed the snow high in the air; then the light could not be seen until the snow fell. Then the man tossed the snow again. So the light kept appearing and disappearing. Close to the house was a large ball of fire. The boy stopped and began to plan how to steal the ball of light.

Then the boy walked up to the man. He said, "Why do you throw up the snow? It hides the light from our village."

The man said, "I am not hiding the light. I am cleaning away the snow. Who are you? Where did you come from? "

The boy said, "It is so dark at our village I do not want to stay there. I came here to live with you."

"All the time?" asked the man.

"Yes," said the boy.

The man said, "All right. Come into the house with me."

Then he dropped his shovel on the ground. He stooped down to lead the way through the underground passage into the house. He let the curtain fall in front of the door as he passed, because he thought the boy was close beside him.

Then the boy caught up the ball of light. He put it in the turned-up flap of his fur coat. Then he picked up the shovel and ran away toward the north. He ran until his feet were tired. Then he put on his raven coat and flew away. He flew rapidly to the north. Raven could hear the man shriek behind him. The man was pursuing him. But Raven flew faster. Then the man cried, "Keep the light; but give me my shovel."

Raven said, "No, you cannot have your shovel. You made our village dark." So Raven flew faster.

Now as Raven flew, he broke off a little piece of the light. This made day. Then he went on a long time in darkness, until he broke off another piece of light.

Thus it was day again. So as Raven flew to the village he broke off the pieces of light. When Raven reached the kashim of his own village he threw away the last piece. He went into the kashim and said to the shamans, " I have brought back the light. It will be light and then dark, so as to make day and night."

After this Raven went out upon the ice because his home was on the seacoast. Then a great wind arose, and the ice drifted with him across the sea to the land on the other side.

Thus Raven brought back the light. It is night and day, as he said it would be. But sometimes the nights are very long because Raven traveled a long way without throwing away a piece of the light.

CHAPTER SIX
RAVEN'S MARRIAGE

Inuit

After Raven had lived alone a long while, he decided to get married. It was late in the fall and the birds were flying southward. So Raven flew away in the path of the geese and birds on their way to summerland. Raven stopped directly in the path.

Soon Raven saw a young goose coming near. He looked down at his feet and called, " Who will marry me? I am a very nice man." The goose flew on.

Soon a black brant passed. Raven looked down at his feet and called, "Who will marry me? I am a very nice man." The black brant flew on. Raven looked after her. He said, "What kind of people are these? They do not even stop to listen."

A duck came near. Raven hid his face and called, "Who will marry me? I am a very nice man." The duck looked toward him, then flew on. Raven said, "Ah, I came very near it then. I shall succeed this time." Soon a whole family of white-front geese came along.

There were the parents, four brothers, and a sister. Raven called out, "Who wants to marry me? I am a fine hunter. I am young and handsome." The geese alighted just beyond him. Raven thought, "Now I will get a wife."

Raven saw near him a pretty white stone with a hole in it. He picked it up, strung it on a long grass stem, and hung it about his neck. Then he pushed up his beak so that it slid to the top of his head like a mask; so he became a dark-colored young man. Then he walked up to the geese. Each of the geese pushed up its bill in the same manner; they became nice looking people. Raven liked the girl; he gave her the stone, thus choosing her for his wife, and she hung it about her own neck. Then all pushed down their bills again and became birds. So they flew south toward the summerland.

The geese flapped their wings heavily and flew slowly. Raven, on outspread wing, glided on ahead. The geese looked after him, saying, " How light and graceful he is! "

When Raven became tired he said, "We had better stop early and look for a place to sleep." Soon they were all asleep.

The next morning the geese were awake early. They wanted to be off. Raven was sound asleep. Father Goose wakened him. He said, "We must make haste. It will snow here soon. We cannot wait."

So the geese flapped their wings and flew slowly and heavily along. Raven led the others with outspread wings. He was always above or ahead of the others. They said, "See how light and graceful he is!"

Thus they travelled until they came to the seashore. They feasted upon the berries on the bushes around it. Soon they were asleep.

Early the next morning the geese made ready to go without breakfast. Raven was hungry but the geese would not wait. As they flapped their wings and started, Father Goose said, " We will stop once on the way to rest; then our next flight will bring us to the other shore." Raven began to be afraid, but he was ashamed to say so.

The geese flapped their wings slowly and flew steadily, heavily along. Raven, with outspread wings, glided ahead. After a long time Raven began to fall behind. His wings ached. The geese flew steadily on. Raven flapped heavily along, then glided on his outstretched wings. But he grew more and more tired. He fell farther and farther behind. At last the geese looked back. Father Goose said, " He must be tired. I thought he was light and active. We will wait."

The geese settled close together in the water. Raven flew slowly up, gasping for breath. He sank down upon their backs. When Raven had his breath again, he put his hand on his breast. He said, " I have an arrow here from an old war. It pains me greatly. That is why I fell behind."

After resting, the geese rose from the water. They flapped slowly along. Raven flew with them. After a while, Raven began to fall behind. He grew more and more tired. At last the geese looked back. Father Goose said, "He must be tired. We will wait." So the geese sank down together in the water, while Raven flew slowly up to them and sank down upon their backs.

Raven said, "I have an arrowhead which pierced my heart in an old war. That is why I fell behind." Raven's wife put her hand on his breast. She could feel it beating like a hammer; she said she could not feel an arrowhead.

So the geese rose again from the water. They flapped slowly along. But Raven's wings were very tired. Before long he fell behind again. Again the geese waited for him.

Then the Geese Brothers began to talk among themselves. They said, "We do not believe he has an arrowhead in his heart. How could he live? "

Now this last time when they rested, they could see the far-off shore. Father Goose said to Raven, " We will not wait for you again. We will not rest again until we reach the shore."

So the geese rose from the water and flapped slowly along. Raven's wings seemed very heavy. The geese flew nearer and nearer the shore ; but Raven flew nearer and nearer the waves. As he came close to the water he shrieked to his wife, " Leave me the white stone. Throw the white stone back to me." It was a magic stone. Thus Raven cried. Then he sank down into the water, but the geese had reached the land.

Raven tried to rise from the water. His wings would not spread. Raven drifted back and forth with the waves. The white caps of the surf buried him. Only once in a while could he get his beak above the water to breathe. Then a great wave cast him on the shore. Then he struggled up the beach. He reached some bushes where he pushed up his beak. Thus he became a small, dark-colored man. Then he took off his raven coat and mask. He hung them on a bush to dry. Raven made a fire drill out of dry wood and made a fire. Thus he dried himself.

CHAPTER SEVEN
RAVEN AND THE MARMOT

Inuit

Once Raven was flying over a reef near the seashore, near seabirds that were perched on the rocks. Seabirds cried to him, " Oh, you offaleater! Oh, you carrion-eater! Oh, you black one!" Raven turned and flew far away crying, "Qaq! qaq! qaq! "He flew far away across the great water until he came to a mountain on the other side.

Raven saw just in front of him the hole of Marmot. Then Raven stood by the door watching, until Marmot came home, bringing food. But Marmot could not enter his hole because Raven stood in the way. Marmot asked Raven to stand to one side. Raven said, "No. They called me ' carrion-eater.' Now I will show them I am not. I will eat you."

Marmot said, " All right; but I have heard that you are a very fine dancer. Now, if you will dance, I will sing. Then you can eat me, but let me see you dance before you eat me."

Raven agreed to dance. Then Marmot sang, "Oh, Raven, Raven, Raven, how well you dance! Oh, Raven, Raven, Raven, how well you dance!"

Raven danced. Then they stopped to rest.

Marmot said, "I like your dancing. Now I will sing again, so shut your eyes and dance your best."

So Raven shut his eyes and danced clumsily around.

Marmot sang, "Oh, Raven, Raven, Raven, what a graceful dancer! Oh, Raven, Raven, Raven, what a fool you are! "

Because Marmot, with a quick run, had darted between Raven's legs and was safe in his hole.

When Marmot was safe in his hole, he put out the tip of his nose and mocked Raven. He said, "Chi- kik-kik, chi-kik-kik, chi-kik-kik! You are the greatest fool I ever saw. What a comical figure you cut when dancing! I could hardly keep from laughing. Just look at me — see how fat I am. Don't you wish you could eat me? "

Raven, in a rage, flew far away.

CHAPTER EIGHT
RAVEN AND THE SEALS

Tsimshian

As Raven traveled along, he came to a house where a man lived near the edge of the water. Raven said to him, "I will be your friend."

The man said, "That is good."

Now the beach in front of the house was full of seals. Raven ate them all during two nights. He ate all the seals in front of the house. Then he was hungry again.

Raven killed the man. Then he used his canoe and harpoon. Raven used those. He speared four seals. Then he returned to the shore. He took the seals out of the canoe and began cutting wood.

Then he built a fire and placed stones in it in order to heat them. Afterward he put the seals on a pile of hot stones. He cooked the four seals and covered them with skunk cabbage leaves.

Raven then raised the cover and took out a seal. He ate it. Then he stretched out his hand and took another seal.

Now there was Stump sitting nearby. Raven held the seal in his hands and said to the stump, "Don't you envy me, Stump?" Then he went into the woods. At once Stump arose and sat down on the hole in which the seals were steaming. The seals were right under Stump.

Then Raven returned, carrying leaves of skunk cabbage.

When he saw Stump sitting on his seals, he cried. He was much troubled because he was hungry. Then he took a stick and dug the ground. He cried all the time he was digging. He found a little bit of meat and ate that. But he could not do anything. He cried all the time because he was so hungry.

CHAPTER NINE
RAVENAND PITCH

Tsimshian

Raven went travelling through the woods until he came to the house of Little Pitch. Little Pitch was rich, and invited him in. When Raven had eaten enough, he slept. When he awakened, he said they would go to catch halibut.

Little Pitch was willing, but said, "It is not good for me to be out after sunrise. I must return while it is still chilly. I shall have enough by that time."
Raven said, " I shall do whatever you say, Chief."

Little Pitch said, "Well!"

Then they started for the fishing place. They fished all night. When the sun rose Little Pitch wanted to go ashore.

Raven said, "I enjoy the fishing. Lie down in the bow of the canoe and cover yourself with a mat."

Little Pitch did so. After a while Raven called, "Little Pitch!"

He answered, "Heh!"

After a while Raven called again, "Little Pitch!"

He answered again in a loud voice.

Again after some time, Raven called again, "Little Pitch!"

Then Little Pitch's answer was very weak because the sun was getting warm. Now Raven hauled up his line and paddled home. He pretended to paddle hard, but he only put his paddles into the water edgewise. Again he called, "Little Pitch!"

"Heh!" Little Pitch replied, but his voice was very weak. The sun was getting still hotter. Then Raven knew that Little Pitch was melting.

Behold! Pitch came out and ran over the halibut in the boat. Therefore the halibut is black on one side.
Then Raven took the pitch and mended his boat with it.

CHAPTER TEN
RAVEN'S DANCING BLANKET

Tsimshian

One day Raven put on the shaman's blanket of his grandfather. Then he went away; he strayed off. He was very poor and he tore his dancing blanket. Then he caught ravens. He used anything to kill the ravens. Then he took the skins of the ravens and tied them together. Then he walked about in them, dressed very well.

Now he saw a good shaman's blanket like the one he had before. He tore his raven's blanket. He took the dancing blanket that hung before him. Behold! It was not a shaman's blanket. It was only the lichens on a tree. Now he saw it was only lichens. He sat down and wept. He took his old raven's blanket and tied it together. Then once more he went on, weeping with hunger.

CHAPTER ELEVEN
RAVEN AND THE GULLS

Tsimshian

Raven did another thing. He induced the olachen to come to Nass River. He said to them, "Go up on both sides of the river." They did so. Then Raven's canoe was quite full of fish. He had not used his rake, but the whole shoal of olachen jumped into his canoe.

Then he camped at Crab-apple place. He clapped on the top of the stone. Then very slippery became the top of that stone that the olachen should not be lost. He put olachen on spits to roast them.

Raven called, "Little Gull!"

Then many gulls came. They ate all the olachen of Raven. They said, " Qana, qana, qana, qana! " They talked much while they ate all the olachen of Raven.

Then Raven was sad. Therefore he took the gulls and threw them into the fireplace. So the tips of their wings have been black, ever since that day.

CHAPTER TWELVE
RAVEN AND THE COOT

Athapascan

Along time ago, Raven wanted all the birds to look well, so he painted them. Raven painted Coot last. Then Coot began to paint Raven, who wanted many bright colors. So Coot painted Raven with bright colors with one hand, but in the other hand he hid charcoal. When Raven looked away, Coot quickly blackened all the bright colors with charcoal. Then Raven was angry and he chased Coot. But Coot ran too quickly, so Raven threw white mud at him, — white mud which spattered over Coot. Therefore Coot had white spots on his head and back. But Coot flew away and left Raven all black.

CHAPTER THIRTEEN
THE ORIGIN OF THE TIDES

Athapascan- Tsetsaut

Along time ago, a man wandered down the Nass River. Wherever he camped, he made rocks of curious shapes. Now his name was Qa, the Raven. The Tlingit call him Yel.

Qa wandered all over the world. At last he traveled westward. Now at that time the sea was always high.

In the middle of the world Qa discovered a rock in the sea. He built a house under the rock. Then he made a hole through it and through the earth and fitted a lid to it. Raven put a man in charge of the hole. Twice a day he opens the lid and twice each day he closes it. When the hole is open the water rushes down through it into the depth then it is ebb tide. When he closes the lid, the water rises again then it is flood tide.

Once upon a time, Tael, a Tlingit chief, while hunting sea otters was carried out to Qa's rock by the tide. The current was so strong he could not escape. When Tael was drawn toward the rock, he saw a few small trees growing on it. Tael threw his canoe line over one of the trees. Thus he escaped being carried down by the water into the hole under the rock. After some time he heard a noise. The man was putting the lid on the hole. Then the water began to rise. Tael paddled rapidly away. He paddled away until the tide began to ebb again. Then he fastened his canoe to a large stone nearby, and waited until flood tide came again. Thus Tael escaped.

CHAPTER FOURTEEN
HOW RAVEN STOLE THE LAKE

Haida

After Raven had made the crows black because they had eaten his salmon — crows had always been white before that, they say — he met some people with feathers on their heads and gambling- stick bags on their backs. They said, "What is the matter?"

Raven said, "Oh, my father and mother are dead."

Then they started home with him. These were the Beavers, they say. They were going out to gamble, but turned back on account of him.

The next morning they put their gambling-stick bags upon their backs and started off again. Raven flew around behind a screen. Lo, a lake lay there! In a creek flowing from it was a fish trap. The fish trap was so full of salmon it looked as if someone were shaking it. There were plenty of salmon in it and in the lake were very small canoes passing each other. Several points of land were red with cranberries.

Raven pulled out the fish trap, folded it together, and laid it down at the edge of the lake. Then he rolled it up with the lake and house, put them under his arm, and pulled himself up into a tree that stood close by. They were not heavy for his arm. He had rolled the lake up just as though it were a blanket. Raven sat in the tree half-way up.

After a while someone came. His house and the lake were not there. After he had looked about him for some time, he looked up. Lo, there sat Raven with their property!

Then the Beavers went quickly to that tree. They began cutting it with their teeth. When it began to fall, Raven went to another one. When that began to fall, he went to another. After the Beavers had cut down many trees in this way, they gave it up. They then traveled about for a long time, they say. After a long time, they found a lake and settled down on it.

Then after Raven had traveled around for a while with the lake, he came to a large open place. He unrolled the lake there. There it lay. He did not let the fish trap or the house go. He kept them to teach the Seaward (mainland) people and the Shoreward (Queen Charlotte Islands) people, they say.

CHAPTER FIFTEEN
RAVEN AND THE FOG WOMAN

Tlingit

Raven wanted to get married. He went to the chief called Fog-Over-The-Salmon, who had a young daughter of marriageable age. The chief was glad that Raven wanted to marry his daughter, but he said,

"You must promise to treat my daughter well. You must have respect for her, and look after her. If you behave badly, she will leave you and you won't get her back."

Raven agreed to what the chief demanded, and the couple was soon married. They lived contentedly in the village near the water all summer and fall. Then winter came, and they were without food.

One, bleak rainy day, after they had been hungry for some time, Raven's wife started making a basket.

"What are you making a basket for?" asked Raven testily. "We have nothing to put in it."

His wife did not answer him, but continued making the basket, until it was very big.

That night they went to sleep hungry again, and the next morning when Raven woke up, he saw his wife sitting on the floor washing her hands in the basket. He got up to look at what she was doing, and when she had finished, there were salmon in the basket! These were the first salmon ever created.

Raven and his wife were very glad, and they cooked and ate the salmon. Every day, she did the same thing: she

75

washed her hands in the basket, and when she had finished, there were salmon in it. Soon, their house was full of drying salmon, and they had plenty to eat.

After a while, however, Raven forgot that he owed his good fortune to his wife. He quarreled with her. Every day they would exchange bad words with one another; and in the end Raven got so angry that he hit his wife on the shoulder with a piece of dried salmon! He had forgotten the words of his father-in-law, the chief.

Raven's wife ran away from him. He chased her, but when he tried to catch hold of her, his hands passed right through her body as if through mist. She ran on, and every time Raven clutched her body, there was nothing to hold on to. He closed his hands on emptiness.

Then she ran into the water, and all the salmon she had dried followed her. Her figure became dim and she slowly disappeared into the mist. Raven, could not catch her, because she was the fog.

Raven went to his father-in-law, Chief Fog-Over-The-Salmon, and begged to have his wife returned. But his father-in-law looked at him sternly, and said, "You promised me that you would have respect for my daughter and take care of her. You did not keep your promise. Therefore, you cannot have her back."

*See "Raven Turns Himself into a Woman" for the continuation of the story

CHAPTER SIXTEEN
RAVEN TURNS HIMSELF INTO A WOMAN

Tlingit

http://www.ankn.uaf.edu/IKS/Subsistence/Tlingit/ravensgr
eed.html

Introduction- Raven has lost his wife, the Fog Woman. He wants to get married again, so that people will look after him, and he won't have to work hard for his food. This time he decides to turn himself into a woman and become a wife.

Raven is lazy and a bad wife: She steals from the Killerwhale people in the village where she lives. Then she decides to kill her husband and all the Killerwhales in the village.

"Raven turns himself into a woman"

Now Raven started on from this place crying, "My wife, my wife!"

Coming to some trees, he saw a lot of gum on one of them and said to the tree, "Why, you are just like me. You are in the same state." For he thought that the tree was crying, just as Raven was crying for his lost wife the Fog Woman.

Raven went to another place and turned himself into a woman. Then she (for Raven was a woman now) thought to herself, "I must get married and have someone to look after me. But to get a husband, I must say my father was a great chief. Whose daughter shall I say I am?"

She looked around thoughtfully, and her eyes rested on a seagull sitting on a high rock. In those days, a chief would always pick out a high place in the village, and would sit there in the morning. The seagull sitting on the high rock reminded her of a chief, so she decided, "I will call the seagull my father. From now on I will call myself Sitter-on-the-High-Cliff's daughter!"

Sometime later, a canoe came along filled with men of the Killerwhale clan who were returning to their village. Raven waved to them, talked to them, and finally convinced one of them to marry her.

The canoe continued on its journey, with Raven a long this time. When it approached the village, a man on the beach saw it coming and shouted out, "Where is your canoe coming from?"

One of the Killerwhales in the canoe replied, "We have been after a wife, and we have her!"

"Which chief's daughter is she?" people asked when the Killerwhales arrived in the village. They knew that Raven must be a chief's daughter, for in those days people never went to fetch a woman by canoe unless she were the daughter of a chief.

"It is Sitter-on-the-High-Cliff's daughter," the Killerwhales replied. And all the villagers believed this.

Raven made herself at home in the Killerwhales' house. Soon, the Killerwhales began to notice that their food was disappearing very rapidly, even though they were always out fishing and hunting, and had their house piled full with boxes of grease.

They wondered to each other, "What is wrong? What has become of all the grease and fat in these boxes?" They could not find out for a long time.

Raven wore a labret in her lip in those days. It was set with abalone shell and was very valuable. One day, the Killerwhales found this labret in one of the boxes of grease and said, "Just look at this labret here in this box. We know who it belongs to!" And they went to Raven and asked her how the labret got into the box.

Raven exclaimed, "Oh, my labret! That's always the way with my labret. Whenever it feels like doing so, it will leave my lip and go off anywhere it chooses!"

For the moment, the Killerwhale people believed Raven.

By and by, Raven said to the Killerwhales, "I wonder what is wrong that I have such bad dreams. I dreamed that all the people in this village were asleep, and my husband went to sleep too and never woke up. My dreams always come true. Whatever I dream will surely happen."

The people looked at each other with frightened eyes.

Late the next night, Raven got a stick, sharpened the ends, crept to where her husband slept, and killed him!

Early the next morning, the village people woke and heard her crying, "Oh, my husband! My husband!" Raven told the people that her husband's last words had been, "When I'm dead take my body to a place some distance from the town". The Killerwhale people did this.

Then Raven said, "When you hear me crying, I don't want any of you to pass the place where I am mourning for him. Leave me alone to cry in peace. Now, tie up the fingers of my right hand, so that may eat with my left hand only. You people must wait on me. You must bring me everything I eat. Also paint my face black."

As she was a widow, they had to do everything just as she told them. These are the rules that people have observed from that time.

Raven stayed there pretending to be mourning for a long time. She was fed by the Killerwhales and had a very easy life for a time. And whenever anyone heard her crying near the spot where her husband's body had been laid no one dared to go near. She lived there a long time, crying. But really she was crying for joy, because she intended to kill all the Killerwhales.

CHAPTER SEVENTEEN
RAVEN AND THE FISH HAWK

Tlingit

http://www.ankn.uaf.edu/IKS/Subsistence/Tlingit/ravensgr
eed.html

After that Raven began to travel. One day he came upon a Fish Hawk. "Oh, my friend!" cried Raven, as if the hawk were his dearest friend. Raven entered Fish Hawk's house, looked around and saw a great amount of food. He smiled broadly when he saw the food.

Raven said to the Fish hawk, "I will stay with you all winter! We will be partners and share our work and our food!" Fish Hawk agreed.

Raven stayed and stayed; but after a while. Fish hawk became very tired of his visitor. Raven shared the food all right, but he did not share in the work!

When Raven noticed that Fish hawk was becoming weary of him, he said, "The time for me to work hasn't come yet. When it's my turn to work, you'll have plenty of rest. You won't have to do a thing! This beach will be covered with all kinds of fish. There will be so much fish; you'll get tired of eating it!"

Fish hawk believed what Raven said. He started thinking about all the things Raven would do for him, and he forgot about how lazy Raven had shown himself to be. He let Raven stay at his house.

Meanwhile, as he was waiting for Raven to be ready to start working, Fish hawk was working all time harder to supply his guest with food. Once in a while he would get angry at Raven all over again for not sharing in the work.

Then Raven would say, "I remember when we first met, Fish Hawk. I was very impressed by you, for I knew then that you were a very wealthy person -- and now I see that I was correct! You are very wealthy and deserve all my respect!" Fish Hawk was pleased. He forgot about his anger. Clever Raven knew how to use flattery!

Still, Raven stayed on and on. And he ate more and more.

But he never kept his promise; he never did any work. He never brought home food.

Then one day the little hawk decided he had had enough. He refused to feed Raven any more. He left his house and he left Raven to find his own food!

The man who told the story you've just read said this about it: "This is the way it is nowadays with persons who have no respect for themselves. They go from house to house to be fed by others. Such persons are greedy, great eaters and lazy.

"People tell their children that those who lead this kind of life are not respected. A person who tells the truth is always known because he keeps his word. There was a boy I knew who wouldn't do anything. They used to say to him,

"You are so lazy that you will be left in some village all alone!"

"That is why the Tlingit tried hard to earn their living and make things comfortable for themselves."

CHAPTER EIGHTEEN
THE FLOOD

Tlingit

Long, long ago, in the days of the animal people, Raven-at-the-head-of-Nass became angry. He said, "Let rain pour down all over the world. Let people die of starvation." At once it be- came so stormy people could not get food, so they began to starve. Their canoes were also broken up, their houses fell in upon them, and they suffered very much. Then Nas-ca-ki-yel, Raven-at-the-head-of-Nass, asked for his jointed dance hat. When he put it on water began pouring out of the top of it. It is from Raven that the Indians obtained this kind of a hat.

When the water rose to the house floor, Raven and his mother climbed upon the lowest retaining timber. This house we are speaking of, although it looked like a house to them, was really part of the world. It had eight rows of retaining timbers.

When Raven and his mother climbed to a higher timber, the people of the world were climbing into the hills. Then Raven and his mother climbed to the fourth timber; by that time the water was half-way up the mountains. When the house was nearly full of water, Raven's mother got into the skin of a cax. To this very day Tlingits do not eat the cax because it was Raven's mother. Then Raven got into the skin of a white bird with copper-colored bill. Now the cax is a diver and stayed upon the surface of the water. But Raven flew to the very highest cloud and hung there by his bill. But his tail was in the water.

After Raven had hung in the cloud for days and days — nobody knows how long — he pulled his bill out and prayed to fall on a piece of kelp. He thought the water had gone down. When Raven fell upon the kelp and flew away he found the waters just half-way down the mountains.

Raven flew around until he met a shark, which had been swimming around with a long stick. Raven took the stick and climbed down it as a ladder to the bottom of the ocean. But Raven had set Eagle to watch the tide.

Raven wandered around the bottom of the ocean until he came to an old woman. He said to her, "How cold I am after eating those sea urchins." He repeated this over and over again.

At last the woman said, "What low tide is this Raven talking about?" Raven did not answer. The woman kept repeating, "What low tide are you talking about?"

Then Raven became angry. He said, "I will stick these sea urchins into you if you don't keep quiet." At last he did so.

Then the woman began singing, "Don't, Raven ! The tide will go down if you don't stop."

But the water was receding, as Raven had told it to, in his magic words. Raven asked Eagle, who was watching the tide, "How far down is the tide now? "

"The tide is as far down as half a man."

"How far down is the tide?" he asked again.

"The tide is very low," said Eagle.

Then the old woman started her magic song again.

Raven said, "Let it get dry all around the world."

After a while, Eagle said, "The tide is very low now. You can hardly see any water."

Raven said, "Let it get still drier."

At last everything was dry. This is the lowest tide there ever was. All the salmon, and whales, and seals lay on the sands because the water was so low. Then the people killed them for food. They had enough food to last them a long time.

When the tide began to rise again, the people were frightened. They feared there would be another flood, so they carried their food back a long distance. Afterward Raven returned to Nass River and found that people there had not changed their ways. They were dancing and feasting. They asked Raven to join them.

CHAPTER NINETEEN
HOW THE RIVERS WERE FORMED

Tlingit

Petrel was the first person created by Raven-at-the-head-of-Nass. He was keeper of the fresh water. No one else might touch it. Now the spring he owned was on a rocky island called Dekino, Fort-far-out, where the well may still be seen. Raven stole a great mouthful of water, but as he flew over the country drops spilled out of his beak. These drops made the rivers: the Nass, Skeena, Stikine, and Chilkat. Raven said, "The water that I drop down upon the earth, here and there, will whirl all the time. There will be plenty of water, but it will not flood the world."

Now before this time, Raven was pure white. But when he stole the water from Petrel he tried to fly out of the smoke hole. Petrel cried, "Spirits of the smoke-hole, hold him fast." **So the smoke-hole spirits held Raven until the smoke blackened his white coat.**

CHAPTER TWENTY
ORIGIN OF FIRE

Tlingit

Long ago, in the days of the animal people, Raven saw a fire far out at sea. He tied a piece of pitch to Chicken Hawk's bill. He said, "Go out to the fire, touch it with the pitchwood, and bring it back." Chicken Hawk did so. The fire stuck to the pitchwood and he brought it back to Raven. Then Raven put the fire into the rock and into the red cedar. Then he said, "Thus shall you get your fire — from this rock and from this red cedar." The tribes did as he told them.

CHAPTER TWENTY ONE
HOW THE DURATOIN OF WINTER CAME TO BE

Tlingit

Once Raven went to the Ground-hog's house for the winter. Now Ground-hogs go into their holes in September. At home they live like people. People to them are animals.

So Raven spent the winter with the Ground-hog and became very tired of it. But he could not get out. Ground-hog enjoyed himself, but Raven acted like a prisoner. Raven kept shouting, "Winter come on. Winter come on." Raven thought that the Ground-hog had power to shorten the winter.

Now at that time, Ground-hog had to stay in his hole for six months; at that time, Ground-hog had six toes, one for each month of winter. Then Raven pulled one toe off each foot, so that the winter would be shorter. That is why the Ground-hog now has but five toes.

CHAPTER TWENTY TWO
RAVEN'S BIG FEAST

Tlingit

Raven's mother died, so he gave a great feast, but first he went to the Ground-hog people to get food. Now the Ground-hog people know when slides descend from the mountains, and they know that spring is then near at hand, so they throw all of their winter food out of their burrows. Raven wanted them to do this. He said, "There is going to be a world snow slide." Ground-hog chief answered, "Well, nobody in this town knows about it."

In the spring when the snow slides did come, the Ground-hogs threw out all their green herbs, and their roots from their burrows.

Therefore Raven said to the people, "I am going to have a feast. I am going to invite the whole world." Raven was going to invite everyone because he had heard that the Gonaqadet had a Chilkat blanket and a Chilkat hat and he wanted to see them. First he invited the Gonaqadet and afterward the other chiefs of all the tribes in the world. At the right time they came.

When the Gonaqadet came in he had on his Chilkat hat with many crowns and his Chilkat blanket, but he was surrounded by a fog. Inside of the house, however, the fog melted away.

Because Raven had this feast, people now have to have feasts. Because Raven had this burial feast, when a man is going to have a burial feast he has a many-crowned hat carved on the top of the dead man's grave post.

CHAPTER TWENTY THREE
RAVEN CREATES THE PORCUPINE

Tlingit

Raven went into the woods and set out to make porcupines. For quills he took pieces of yellow cedar bark. These he set all the way up and down the porcupines back so that bears would be afraid of it. That is why bears never eat porcupines. Raven said to the porcupine, "Whenever anyone comes near you, throw your tail about." That is why people are afraid to go near a porcupine.

CHAPTER TWENTY FOUR
HOW RAVEN TAUGHT THE CHILKAT
PEOPLE

Tlingit

Raven taught the Chilkats that there were Athapascan Indians. He went back into their country. So the Chilkat people to this day make their money by going there. Raven also taught the Chilkats how to make secret storehouses outside of their villages, and he taught them how to put salmon into the storehouses and keep them frozen over winter. That is how the Chilkats got their name, from toil, "storehouse," and xat, "salmon."

Raven also showed the Chilkats the first seeds of Indian tobacco and taught them how to plant it. After the tobacco was grown, he dried it and pounded it up with burned clam shells. The Chilkats made a great deal of money by trading tobacco with the Athapascans.

Afterward Raven went beyond Copper River to Yukatat. There he showed the people how to make canoes out of skins.

CHAPTER TWENTY FIVE
THE LAND OTTER AND THE RAVEN

Tlingit

Raven said to the Land Otter, "You will live in the water just as well as on land." Raven and the Land Otter were good friends, so they went halibut-fishing together. Land Otter was a good fisherman. Raven said to the Land Otter, "You will always have your house on a point where there are breezes from all sides. Whenever a canoe with people capsizes, you will save the people and make them your friends." That is how the Land Otter Man was created: because Raven told this to the Land Otter.

If people who are taken away by Land Otters are brought back by their friends, they become shamans. It was through the Land Otters that shamans were first known. Shamans, by means of Land Otter spirits, can see each other, even though others cannot.

CHAPTER TWENTY SIX
HOW DAYLIGHT CAME TO THE NASS RIVER

Tlingit

When Raven had grown quite large he walked down the bank of the Nass River one day, until he heard the noise people were making in the darkness as they fished for olachen. Now all the people in the world lived at one place on the Nass River. They had heard that Raven-at-the-head-of-Nass had something called "daylight." They were afraid of it and talked about it a great deal.

Raven shouted to the fishermen, "Why do you make so much noise? If you make so much noise I will bring the daylight here."

Eight canoe-loads of people were fishing there. They said, "You are not Nascakiyel. You are not Raven-at-the-head-of-Nass. How can you have the daylight?" They kept on making much noise.

Then Raven opened the box and daylight shot over the world like lightning. They made still more noise. So Raven opened the box wide and there was daylight everywhere.

Then the people were frightened. Some ran into the woods and some jumped into the water. Those that had clothes of fur seal skins jumped into the water; they became seals. Those which had clothing of bear skins, marten skins, and wolf skins, ran into the woods and turned into grizzly bears, martens, and wolves.

CHAPTER TWENTY SEVEN
RAVEN GIVES NAMES TO THE BIRDS

Tlingit

Now Raven went around among the birds, teaching them. He said to the Grouse, "You are to live in a place where it is wintry. You will always live in a place high up so you will have plenty of breezes." Then Raven gave the Grouse four white pebbles. He said, "You will never starve so long as you have these four pebbles."

Raven also said to the Grouse, "You know that the Sea-lion is your grandchild. You must get four more pebbles and give them to him." That is why the sea-lion has four large pebbles. It throws these at hunters. If one strikes a person, it kills him. From this story it is known that the Grouse and the Sea-lion understand each other.

Raven said to the Ptarmigan, "You will be the maker of snowshoes. You will know how to travel in snow." It was from these birds that the Athapascans learned how to make snowshoes, and how to put the lacings on.

Raven came next to the Wild Canary that lives all the year around in the Tlingit country. He said, "You will be head among the very small birds. You are not to live on the same food as human beings. Keep away from them."

Then Raven said to the Robin, "You will make people happy by your whistle. You will be a good whistler."

Then Raven said to Kun, the Flicker, "You will be chief among the birds of your size. You will not be found in all places. You will seldom be seen."

Raven said to the Lugan, a bird that lives far out on the ocean, "You will seldom be seen near shore. You will live on lonely rocks, far out on the ocean."

When Raven came to Snipes, he said, "You will always go in flocks. You will never go out alone." Therefore we always see snipes in flocks.

Raven said to the Asqacatci, a small bird with yellow-green plumage, " You will always go in flocks. You will always be on the tree tops. That is where your food is."

Raven said to a very small bird, Kotlai, the size of a butterfly, "You will be liked. You will be seen only to give good luck. People will hear your voice, but seldom see you."

Then to the Blue-jay Raven said, "You will have very fine clothes. You will be a good talker. People will take colors from your clothes."

Then Raven said to the Xunkaha, "You will never be seen unless the north wind is going to blow." That is what the name Xunkaha means.

To the Crow, Raven said, "You will make lots of noise. You will be great talkers." That is why, when you hear one crow, you hear a lot of others right afterward.

Raven said to the Gusyiadul, "You will be seen only when warm weather is coming. Never come near except when warm weather is coming."

To the Hummingbird Raven said, "People will enjoy seeing you. If a person sees you once, he will want to see you again."

Raven said to the Eagle, "You will be very powerful and above all birds. Your eyesight will be very good. It will be easy for you to get what you want." Then Raven put talons on the eagle and said they would be useful to him.

Thus Raven taught all the birds.

DENNIS WALLER

CHAPTER TWENTY EIGHT
THE ORIGIN OF THE WINDS

Tlingit

Now Raven went off to a certain place and created West Wind. Raven said to it, "You shall be my son's daughter. No matter how hard you blow, you shall hurt nobody."

Raven also made South Wind. When South Wind climbs on top of a rock it never ceases to blow.

Raven made North Wind and on top of a mountain he made a house for it with ice hanging down the sides. Then he went in and said to North Wind, "Your back is white." That is why mountains are white with snow.

CHAPTER TWENTY NINE
HOW THE DURATION OF LIFE CAME TO BE

Tlingit

RAVEN-AT-THE-HEAD-OF-NASS tried to make human beings, at the same time, out of a rock and out of a leaf. But he created human beings out of the leaf first. Then Raven showed a leaf to people. He said, "You see this leaf. You are to be like it. When it falls off the branch and rots there is nothing left of it."

That is why there is death in the world. If men had come from the hard rocks there would be no death. Years ago, when people were getting old, they would say, "It is unlucky that we did not come from the rock. We are made from leaves; therefore we must die."

DENNIS WALLER

CHAPTER THIRTY
RAVEN AND THE GHOST TOWN

Tlingit

Once Raven came to a large town which was deserted. Everyone seemed to have died. Raven entered the largest house, but he felt someone continually pushing him away. Yet he saw no one there. It was a ghost house. The place was called Ghost Town.

Raven then loaded a canoe with provisions from the empty houses and started to paddle away. He did not notice that a long rope was fastened to the stern of the canoe and to a tree on the shore. When Raven had paddled the length of the rope, the canoe was pulled right back to the beach. All the provisions were carried back to the houses. Yet Raven could see no one. Then a ghost dropped a large stone on Raven's foot. This made him very lame.

CHAPTER THIRTY ONE
RAVEN SHOWS THE AFTERLIFE

Tlingit

After Raven had created people, a man died. Raven came into his house and saw his wife and children weeping around him. Raven raised with both hands the blanket of the dead man and held it over his body. So he brought him back to life. Now Raven and the man both told the woman there was no death. She would not believe them. Then Raven said to her, "Lie down and go to sleep."

When the woman slept she saw a wide trail. There were many people on it and many fierce animals. Good people had to pass this trail in order to live again. At the end of the trail there was a broad river, and a canoe came to her from the other side. When she crossed the river, people came to her. They said, "You had better go back. We are not in a good place. We are hungry here and can get no water to drink. We are cold."

That is why people burn the bodies of the dead and place food in the fire for them to eat. If they were not burned their spirits would be cold. That is why food and drink are given to them at the feast of the dead.

CHAPTER THIRTY TWO
GONAQADET AND THE ORIGIN OF THE CHILKAT BLANKET

Tsimshian

In the days of the animal people, long, long ago, all the animals were divided into different tribes. In those days also, animals could take off their furry skins; then they looked just like people.

Now in those days long ago, a group of women once went out to search for wild celery in the early spring. They found it growing here and there, and spent all day gathering it. Then they tied it in bundles and started home with it on their backs.

Now among these women was the daughter of a chief. She picked twigs as she followed in the trail in the evening light, and then slipped into the footprints of a brown bear. The jolt loosened her pack. She stopped to readjust her bundle of celery. She said sharp words about bears. Then she hastened on to rejoin her companions who were already lost in the dusk.

Suddenly the chief's daughter heard footsteps behind her. A handsome young man joined her. Soon he asked her to be his wife. The chief's daughter consented, so she went home with him. They walked far, far into the woods until they came to Bear village. Then the chief's daughter knew that her lover belonged to the Bear tribe.

After a while the chief's daughter became unhappy. She wanted to go back to her father's home, but the Bear tribe watched her so she could not escape.

One day chief's daughter reached the shore. Out on the water she saw a fisherman in a boat, and she called to him to rescue her. The fisherman touched his canoe with his killing club and in one bound it sprang to the shore, just as the Bear and some of his tribe appeared. The fisherman began to fight Bear, but he could not kill him. Then the chief's daughter told him to strike Bear between the eyes, because his heart was there. So Bear was killed.

The fisherman took the chief's daughter in his canoe. But behold! — he was no fisherman at all. It was Gonaqadet, the spirit of the sea. So the woman married Gonaqadet, who was very kind to her.

After a long while, the chiefs daughter became unhappy again. She wanted her son to be trained by her people, as the custom was. Then Gonaqadet permitted her to return to earth with the boy, but he made her promise that she would weave him a blanket telling of her life and his courtship. So the woman returned to earth from the sea. Then she wove for Gonaqadet the blanket. This was the first Chilkat blanket.

Now one day Yel, the Raven, wandering along the seashore, entered a great cavern under the sea. There he found Gonaqadet, wearing a beautiful Chilkat blanket. Gonaqadet welcomed Raven, and offered him food. He placed food before him in two long carved platters. After Raven had feasted, Gonaqadet taught him many dances and gave him a copy of the blanket pattern. Then Raven taught the people how to weave the blankets, but he taught the Tsimshian tribe first. Afterward the Chilkats learned how to weave them.

SELECTED BIBLIOGRAPHY

Boas, Franz- Bella Bella Text- Columbia University Press 1928

Boas, Franz - 31st Annual Report of the Bureau of American Ethnology, (Tsimshian mythology. Based on texts recorded by Henry W. Tate) 1909-1910, GPO- Washington 1916

Boas, Franz- The Central Eskimo- GPO- Washington 1888

De Laguna, Frederica – "Tlingit Ideas About the Individual" Southwestern Journal of Anthropology- 1956

Krause, Aurel – "The Tlingit Indians" Translated by Erna Gunther, University of Washington Press- 1956

Judson, Katharine Berry- Myths and Legends of Alaska- A.C. McClurg & Co., Chicago, 1911

Swanton, John R. – Tlingit Myths and Texts. Bulletin 39, Bureau of American Ethnology, Smithsonian Institute, 1909

Waller, Dennis- In Search of the Kushtaka, Amazon.com- 2014

OTHER BOOKS BY DENNIS WALLER

Are You an Indigo? Discover Your Authentic Self

The Art of Talking to Christ, The Theory and Practice of Christian Mysticism

Indigo Wisdom by Francesca Rivera and Dennis Waller

The Tao Te Ching A Translation

Way of the Tao Living an Authentic Life

Hsin Hsin Ming

Zen and Tao, A Little Book on Buddhism Thought and Meditation

Nagarjuna's Tree of Wisdom A Translation

The Importance of the Tao, A Short Essay

The Tao of Kenny Loggins

In Search of The Kushtaka, Alaska's Other Bigfoot: The Land-Otter Man of the Tlingit Indians

Reflections- A Love Story- Part One

9 Keys You Must Master to be a Miserable Asshole

9 Things You Must Know Before Starting a Business

Texas Jack's Famous Pralines Secret Recipe Book

Texas Jack's Famous Sweet Potato Recipes

Texas Jack's Famous Christmas Pie Recipes

Texas Jack's Famous Caramels Secret Recipe Book

EXCERPT FROM "IN SEARCH OF THE KUSHTAKA"

The Kushtaka

What are the Kushtaka?

There are incredible stories of the sinister Kushtaka or "land otter man" as it is known by the Tlingit's all throughout Southeastern Alaska. Whether these stories are the stuff of legend and myth remains to be seen. However a legend that endures over time, endures for a reason, leaving us with the question. Is the legend and myth of the Kushtaka something that really exists? Is it based on actual events or the byproduct of a vivid imagination of a people unable to explain the unexplainable?

The purpose of this book is to explore this amazing mystery, to see if we can unlock the door to the Kushtaka and discover the truth. Joseph Campbell said myths are clues to the spiritual potentialities of the human life, that a myth helps you to put your mind in touch with the experience of being alive. In this case, in order to experience being alive, we might have to experience being scared to death.

The Kushtaka are mystical shape shifting creatures with supernatural powers. They are masters at waging psychological warfare with the ability to twist time and space creating anomalies that defy the laws of physics. It is said they possess telepathic abilities. Their ability to move freely from one place to another in an instant is legendary. Appearing as someone the victim knows is commonplace in the stories of the encounters with the Kushtaka. From deceased relatives, to being a friend, to appearing as a ghostly creature, there are no limits to what or whom the Kushtaka can transform into.

Encounters have told of the unsuspecting victim having their worst nightmares brought to life, as if the Kushtaka were able to draw on the fears of their intended targets. In the worst of reports, the Kushtaka will possess the person and as a malevolent trickster, bring harm to them and those around them, tormenting them to the point of driving them insane, even to the point of death. The Kushtaka seem to have a special hatred for those who do not take them seriously and laugh at the Kushtaka as if it they are a joke. For those folks who fall into this category and venture in the land of the Kushtaka, they will soon find that the Kushtaka has an agenda for them.

The Kushtaka are considered evil and treated with a level of trepidation among the Tlingit. It is believed that the Kushtaka deprived their victims of everlasting life thus not allowing for the victims soul to be reincarnated. These creatures appear to the victims as in the form of relatives or friends to confuse the victim. Their primary purpose is to lure the unsuspecting target away from their homes in order to turn them into Kushtaka. On the seas, the Kushtaka are feared for taking advantage of the Tlingit's in their canoes. They prey on the drowning by expediting the Tlingit's demise by creating these disastrous events.

John Swanton, an American anthropologist and linguist who studied the Tlingit people in the early part of the nineteenth century had this to say about the land otter myth, "Although apparently harmless, the land otter was dreaded more than any other creature. This was on account of their supposed supernatural powers, fondness of stealing people away, depriving them of their senses and turning them into land-otter men. When a person was in danger of drowning, canoes would come to him or her and the people in them would say, "I am your friend," and take the person home. After that he or she became like the land-otter people.

Adding to the mystery is the location of their habitat. The Kushtaka are said to live along the southeastern coast of Alaska, hidden away in the deep rugged rainforest that even today remains mostly uncharted and unknown to man. Protected by rough seas to the west and insurmountable mountains to the east and north, these creatures are literally cut off from the world you and I know. If someone or something wanted to drop off the face of the earth, this is one place where you could do it. With names like the "Bay of Death," it's easy to see how someone could disappear in this lonely vastness, never to be seen again.

Some consider the Kushtaka to be a cousin to Bigfoot while others believe the Kushtaka are multi-dimensional beings. There are no photos or videos, no cast of their footprint. There have been no reports of the Kushtaka named Harry having dining with the Henderson's. Nor has anyone claimed to have a Kushtaka stuffed and mounted. These creatures are much more mysterious, almost as if Stephen King himself created them.

Kushtaka or Kooshdakhaa is a Tlingit word meaning "land otter man." The Kushtaka is on one hand the nemeses of the Tlingit people, yet necessary to their Shamans who play a critical role in the survival of the Tlingits. The Tlingit people are as mysterious in their beliefs as the Kushtaka making for strange bedfellows.

In order to get a better understanding of the Kushtaka we must take a look at a few things. First, we need to explore the Tlingit Indians, whose zest of life is matched only by their insatiable connection to the spirit world. Primarily, we'll examine their Shamans and their mythology. There is an intimate relationship between the two that reveals a much darker and deeper meaning. Is it possible that there is a connection to the Kushtaka, Tlingit Shamans and quantum mechanics? Could this phenomenon be an example of the "Superstring Theory" in practice? Perhaps, this is the sort of behavior one would expect to see in dealing with extra dimensions. Are these Kushtaka from another world, another dimension? I wonder what Michio Kaku, the theoretical physicist, would think about all of this.

In addition to the Tlingit myths, we need to take a look at other myths of indigenous people from around the world. There are strikingly similar creatures throughout these myths that raise the question as to their origins and validity. From Japan to Chile to Alaska, the similarity is striking. Is this just a coincidence or is there more than what meets the eye. Joseph Campbell did a tremendous amount of research and study into myths. We'll see if maybe, there might be an explanation to help shed light on the Kushtaka.

While the Kushtaka might or might not be related to Bigfoot, it is important to take a look at those trying to attain empirical proof to show that such myths do indeed exist. There is a raging debate taking place in the science community on the alleged DNA sequencing of Bigfoot. We have skeptics among those in the field and we'll get to see their point of view as well as those involved in proving their existence.

The most compelling evidence however, if we can use that word, are the firsthand accounts of people who have encountered the Kushtaka. While there might not be a definitive snapshot of the Kushtaka, what does remain is more frightening and terrifying than any photo. Their stories read more like something out of a thrilling horror novel dripping with intrigue, mystery and suspense.

You might find these stories reminiscent of the movie Blair Witch Project or perhaps the movie The Forth Kind. Whatever comparison you draw from reading these stories, I assure you'll most definitely feel their fear and terror. The probable conclusion you will draw from reading their experiences? That reality is in fact, stranger than fiction.

Why the Land Otter?

This is the question, why are the Kushtaka based on the land otters. Within the environment of southeastern Alaska, there isn't any other animal that is perceived to be the most human-like than the land otter. Among the attributes of the otter to consider is the fact that they are one of the most intelligent non-human species on the planet, excellent hunters, known to create tools, playful with human-like characteristics and having an advance social hierarchy and skills.

A remarkable coincidence or is there more to this than meets the eye?

Adding to the mystery, if we look at other beliefs, we see how to Zoroastrians, the otter was considered to be truly pure, therefore, sacred to Ahura Mazda, the uncreated god who represents the highest degree of wisdom, light, and goodness in their pantheon. The Ojibwa Indians have a legend where the otter was entrusted with the secrets of the Midewiwin also known as the Grand Medicine Society, a secretive organization of medicine men, not unlike the shamans of the Tlingit. Least, there is the Tibetan symbol for universal love with the mating of the otter with a fish. Clearly, there is a reverence of the otter stretching across the globe.

However, within the context of the environment in southeastern Alaska and the Tlingit, it isn't a stretch to see the anthropomorphization of the land otter. Especially considering there are no monkeys, apes or gorillas indigenous to this area, much less known to the Tlingit people before the arrival of the Europeans in 1741 followed by the Spanish in 1775.

The land otter has played a major role in the Tlingit society. Economically, this goes back to the days leading up to the nineteenth century when sea otters represented wealth through the hunting of their furs until nearly killed into extinction.

Socially, the land otter is crucial to the Tlingit belief system and their shamans with the land otters representing the symbolic link between the living and the dead. This is brought about by the symbolic aspect of the otter being able to live on land as well as the sea, creating a bridge bringing together the two worlds. This point is stressed in the book by Joseph Campbell, "Hero with a Thousand Faces," The Tlingit see themselves subconsciously in the land otter. The land otter is a mirror reflection of their own ability to be masters of land, sea, and rulers of their domain.

The otters are very fast swimmers, on the surface and underwater, with the ability to remain under for very long periods. Like the otter, the Tlingit are swift on the water in their hand hewed canoes, hunting and fishing for their prey. Like the Tlingit, the otter relies on the water for the mainstay of their diet.

In mythic realms, the otter travels on a "canoe" of the skate fish in their hunt for human souls.

While the relationship between the land otter people and people is adversarial, there are stories where the land otters helped and befriended people in need. The story of Kaka who was taken by the land otters and held for two years tells of his dead aunt who had become a land otter helped him escape. This shows a benevolent nature on behalf of the land otters. Then there is the story of the land otter sister, a woman who had drowned years earlier who came back from the land of the land otters and assisted her brother and his children with food and labor. There are several more stories demonstrating this compassionate side of the land otters.

Interesting, this correlates with the Tlingit belief that dead relatives who reside in the land of the dead are able to assist their love ones when they return to land of the living. Seemly, there is a sense of acquired supernatural powers among the dead who return. Whether this comes from the land otters or another source remains to determine.

One aspect of those who live to tell the tale from the land of the otters are the striking similarities of the two worlds. The stories mention how much the homes, villages, customs, even the hierarchy of chiefs and the poor and rich resemble life on earth.

Why can't we find the Kushtaka?

That is an easy question to answer, especially for the Alaska State Troopers. On average, about 5 out of every 1,000 people are reported missing every year in Alaska, about double the national average. To put that into perspective, that would come out to roughly 93 people a day disappearing in the Dallas-Fort Worth area or over 33,000 thousand people a year.

If that were to happen in the DFW area, it would be national news, creating a mass panic among the population. But in Alaska, it is the norm. Granted, most of the missing person reports are runaways who are found or returned, the fact remains that Alaska has the highest percentage of unsolved missing person reports.

With so much of the terrain unknown and with the sheer vastness of the landscape, the Alaska State Troopers are at a significant disadvantage. When someone does come up missing, the search area can be the size of most states. Another fact to consider is even in the most populated cites in Alaska, you can be only 5 minutes away from complete and utter wilderness. Walk just a mile outside the city limits of Juneau and you might as well be on another planet.

The weather plays a major role in this too. With snow storms that can come up with no warning, leaving a blanket of snow covering up any traces of anyone ever being there. Six months of near darkness, unbelievable cold, more rivers, glaciers and lakes that can be counted plus the wildlife must be taken into consideration. They're countless stories of searchers being just a few feet away from a body, literally walking over the remains of the missing person due to the ice, snow and brush.

What does all of this have to do with finding the Kushtaka? With the odds that the State of Alaska with their state of the art technology won't find you, what makes you think they are going to find someone or something that doesn't want to be found?

Now take into consideration that the Kushtaka are in their natural environment. With the ability to move effortlessly through the forest, to smell and hear humans from miles away, it would stand to reason they could easily outmaneuver and hide from us.

While it stands to reason that the Kushtaka are aggressively trying to avoid being detected, at the same time that aggressiveness could turn into killing in order to protect themselves from being discovered. Maybe the reason there hadn't been any tools or weapons found is the fact the Kushtaka don't need them. This is a species that has evolved in an environment where they have the upper advantage over humans.

Location- Southeastern Alaska

Southeast Alaska, often referred to as the Alaska Panhandle, is the southeastern portion of the U.S. state of Alaska, which lies west from the northern half of the Canadian province, British Columbia. The majority of Southeast Alaska's area is part of the Tongass National Forest, the United States largest national forest. The Tongass National Forest is the largest national forest in the United States at 17 million acres. The region is noted for its scenery and mild rainy climate.

Southeast Alaska is the northern terminus of the Inside Passage, a protected waterway of convoluted passages between islands and fjords, beginning in Puget Sound in Washington State. This was an important travel corridor for Tlingit and Haida Native peoples, as well as gold-rush era steamships. In modern times, it is an important route for the Alaska Marine Highway ferries as well as cruise ships. Southeast Alaska has a land area of 35,138 square miles comprising six entire boroughs and three census areas, in addition to the portion of the Yakutat Borough lying east of 141° West longitude. Although it has only 6.14 percent of Alaska's land area, it is larger than the state of Maine, and almost as large as the state of Indiana. The Southeast Alaskan coast is roughly as long as the west coast of Canada. The 2000 census population of Southeast was 72,954 inhabitants, about 42 percent of whom were concentrated in the city of Juneau.

It includes the Tongass National Forest, Glacier Bay National Park, Admiralty Island National Monument, Misty Fjords National Monument, Alaska's Inside Passage, and myriad large and small islands. The largest islands are, from North to South, Chichagof Island, Admiralty Island, Baranof Island, Kupreanof Island, Revillagigedo Island and Prince of Wales Island. Major bodies of water of Southeast Alaska include Glacier Bay, Lynn Canal, Icy Strait, Chatham Strait, Stephens Passage, Frederick Sound, Sumner Strait, and Clarence Strait.

Southeast Alaska is a temperate rain forest within the Pacific temperate rain forest zone, as classified by the World Wildlife Fund's eco-region system, which extends from northern California to Prince William Sound. The most common tree species are Sitka spruce and western hemlock. Wildlife includes brown bears, black bears, the endemic Alexander Archipelago wolf, Sitka black-tailed deer, humpback whales, orcas, five species of salmon, bald eagles, harlequin ducks, scoters, and marbled murrelets.

Major cities are Juneau, Ketchikan, and Sitka. Other towns are Petersburg, Wrangell, Metlakatla, Haines, Hoonah, Angoon, Kake, Craig, Klawock, Thorne Bay, Yakutat, Skagway, and Gustavus. There are also many towns and villages with +/- 100 people, such as Baranof Warm Springs, Edna Bay, Elfin Cove, Excursion Inlet, Funter Bay, Hyder, Meyers Chuck, Pelican, Port Alexander, Port Frederick, Port Protection, and Tenakee Springs.

This area is the traditional homeland of the Tlingit people, home of a historic settling of Haida, and a modern settlement for the Tsimshian. The region is closely connected to Seattle and the American Pacific Northwest economically and culturally.

Major industries in Southeast Alaska include commercial fishing and tourism (primarily the cruise ship industry). Logging has been an important industry in the past, but has been steadily declining with competition from other areas and the closure of the region's major pulp mills.

Due to the extremely rugged, mountainous nature of Southeastern Alaska, almost all communities (with the exception of Hyder, Skagway, and Haines) have no road connections outside of their locale, so aircraft and boats are the major means of transport. The Alaska Marine Highway passes through this region.

Southeast Alaska is primarily served by the state-run Alaska Marine Highway and secondarily by the Prince of Wales Island-based Inter-Island Ferry Authority. Small companies like Sitka-based Allen Marine and other independent operators in the Lynn Canal occasionally also offer marine passenger service. Ship traffic in the area is seasonally busy with cruise ships.

Alaska Airlines is by far the largest air carrier in the region, with Juneau's Juneau International Airport serving as the aerial hub for all of the Southeast and Ketchikan's Ketchikan International Airport serving as a secondary hub for southern Southeast Alaska. Alaska's bush airlines and air taxis serve many of the smaller and more isolated communities and villages in the regions.

ABOUT THE AUTHOR

Dennis Waller, bestselling author, film maker and speaker, is recognized as an expert on spiritual experience, self-discovery, and exploring the human consciousness. His work on Buddhism, Zen, and the Tao is internationally recognized. His translation of Nagarjuna's Tree of Wisdom is only the second translation into English. He has taught classes on Enochian magic of Doctor John Dee and Sir Edward Kelly, Quantum Physics in relation to Eastern Thought and Philosophy, and Workshops for Indigos.

His current film project, "In Search of the Kushtaka, Alaska's Other Bigfoot: Myth or Reality, The Land-Otter Man of the Tlingit People" is set for release in late fall 2014. Covering the Tlingit and comparative mythologies along with thoughts from the science community and firsthand accounts of encounters with the Kushtaka, this film promises to be an enlightening look into the phenomena known as the Kushtaka.

He may be contacted by email with your questions at dennismwaller@yahoo.com or by mail at

Dennis Waller
PO Box 210442
Bedford, TX 76095

NOTES

NOTES

Printed in Poland
by Amazon Fulfillment
Poland Sp. z o.o., Wrocław